D1742900

101 Essential Windows Tips

Clifton Karnes

COMPUTE Books

Greensboro, North Carolina

Editor: Tony Roberts
Interior Design: The Roberts Group

Printed in the United States of America.

10 9 8 7 6 5 4 3 2 1

ISBN 0-87455-262-1

COMPUTE Books, 324 West Wendover Avenue, Suite 200, Greensboro, North Carolina 27408, is a General Media International Company and is not associated with any manufacturer of personal computers.

Windows is a trademark and Microsoft a registered trademark of Microsoft Corporation.

Contents

Font and Printer Tips

DOS and PIF Tips

Performance Tips

Customization Tips

Power Tips

Introduction

Microsoft Windows is the hottest-selling program in the PC's history. But there's a problem with Windows. It can be difficult to use, and hidden deep inside it are many undocumented features. While the Windows environment unquestionably has power to burn, it's hard to get beneath the interface to tap this power.

This book will make it easy for you to take full advantage of Windows' features. It focuses on shortcuts and enhancements that will propel beginners to power user status and drive power users into the wizard category. You'll find tips on almost every aspect of Windows, including Program Manager, File Manager, accessories, fonts, printers, DOS, performance, and customizing.

To make it as easy as possible to use this book, each tip fills either a single page or two facing pages, and each uses an identical form. At the beginning of each tip, you'll see the tip number and name. Directly below you'll find the problem the tip solves, a short description of its solution, and step-by-step instructions on how to implement the solution. You'll also find illustrations, where necessary, and references to related tips.

Although the book was written using Windows 3.1, almost every tip was tested with 3.0 and can be used with that version, too. Where keystrokes or methods are different for the two versions, these differences are clearly marked.

Also note that all the tips in this book are compatible with 386 enhanced mode, and some—for example, the tips that discuss multitasking DOS programs and using virtual memory—require it. If you're using Windows in standard mode, it should be obvious which tips do not apply.

That's it. Let's get started and have some fun with Windows.

Rename a Program Manager group

While it's easy to rename files, it's not obvious how to rename a group.

Leave the group's filename as it is, but change the description—the name you see in Program Manager.

❶ Minimize the group you want to rename.

❷ Single click on the group with the mouse.

❸ Select File, Properties from the menu bar.

❹ In the Description text box, type in the group's new name.

Windows Setup installs a group called *Non-Windows Applications*. This name is so long it obscures the names of other groups beside it when it's minimized. Changing its name to *DOS Programs* or simply *DOS* will solve this problem.

Install icons on Program Manager fast

Using the Program Manager to install icons can be time consuming, error prone, and tedious.

Drag icons from File Manager to Program Manager.

❶ Make sure Program Manager is active, and minimize all other windows.

❷ Open File Manager (on the Main group).

❸ Double-click on the desktop or press Ctrl-Esc to call Task Manager.

❹ Click on Tile or press Alt-T to arrange File Manager and Program Manager windows side by side.

❺ Drag the files you want to install from File Manager to the Program Manager group.

❻ You can drag any program file (with an EXE, COM, PIF, or BAT extension) or any associated document file.

You can drag files to a Program Manager group window that's maximized, restored, or minimized.

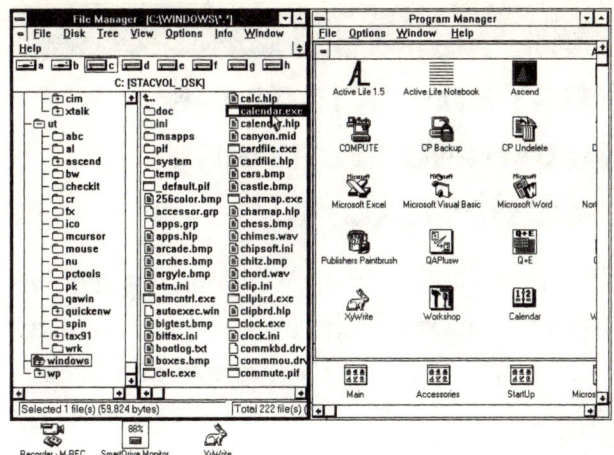

Drag files from File Manager to a group window in Program Manager.

Run any Windows program from any subdirectory

Program Manager runs Windows applications from the directory where the program is located, which is often not the directory you want to be in.

Fool Program Manager into thinking that the program is in a different subdirectory.

Let's say you've created a subdirectory off your Windows directory called WRI for your Windows Write documents, and you want Write to start up in this subdirectory rather than the Windows subdirectory, which is where the Write program file is located.

Windows 3.1:

❶ Select File, Properties.

❷ Type in the name of the directory in which you want to start the application in the Working Directory text box. For our example, you'd type C:\WINDOWS\WRI.

Windows 3.0:

❶ Make sure the application you want to install is on your path (you'll find the PATH statement located in your AUTOEXEC.BAT file). Write is in the WINDOWS subdirectory and, therefore, should be on your path.

❷ In Program Manager, choose File, New, and Program Item.

❸ Put the program's name, in this case WRITE, in the Description text box.

❹ In the Command Line box, type the path to the document's subdirectory followed by the program's name. For our example, you'd use

C:\WINDOWS\WRI\WRITE.EXE.

❺ Program Manager will respond with "Invalid path," but don't worry.

❻ Select the program's icon and choose File, Properties, and press Change Icon.

❼ In the File Name text box, type the full, true path to the application. In our example, you'd type

C:\WINDOWS\WRITE.EXE.

❽ Click on OK in this dialog box and the next one.

When you're typing filenames and paths in Program Manager, or anywhere else in Windows for that matter, case isn't important. In other words, you can type WRITE or Write. Either is correct. I use uppercase to make the examples easier to read.

Move and copy icons from one group to another

Copying and moving icons from one Program Manager group to another is often a necessity, but you don't always get the results you expect.

Move icons by dragging and dropping them, and copy icons by pressing the Control key while dragging and dropping.

❶ To move an icon from one group to another, first make sure both source and destination groups are visible (the destination group can be either restored or minimized).

❷ Click on the icon you want to move and hold down the mouse button (this is normally the left mouse button, unless you've changed the primary button with Control Panel).

❸ While holding down the mouse button, drag the icon to its destination and release the button.

❹ To copy an icon, repeat steps 1 through 3 above, but press the Control key while you drag and drop.

Note that a minimized group can't be an icon on another group.

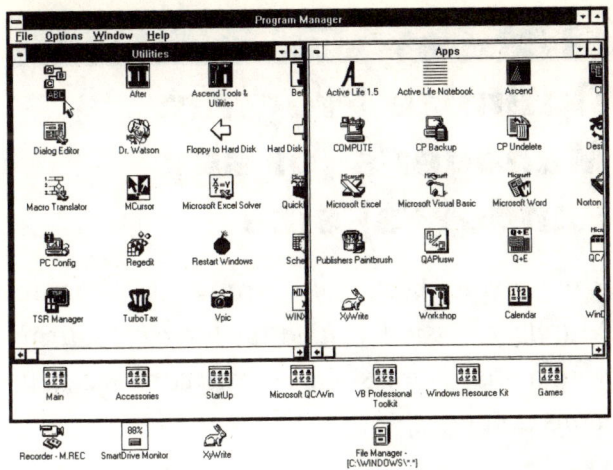

Click and drag an icon to move it from one group to another. Ctrl-click and drag an icon to copy it from one group to another.

Optimize Program Manager's (or any window's) size

Unless you specifically arrange it, Program Manager is usually either too large (obscuring your icons) or too small (so you can't see all its icons and groups).

Use Task Manager to tile Program Manager.

❶ Make sure all applications except Program Manager are minimized (note that you must have at least one minimized application icon on your desktop).

❷ Double-click on the desktop or press Ctrl-Esc to call Task Manager.

❸ Click on Tile or press Alt-T to tile Program Manager's window.

❹ Program Manager will fill the screen except for a band at the bottom that's just tall enough to display minimized icons.

❺ If you like Program Manager's optimized size, be sure to save your changes when you exit Windows.

The Tile command was doubtless intended to
be used with a group of windows—to arrange
them so you could see the maximum of each
one. The fact that Tile works with a single
window makes it ideal for optimizing any
program's window. Just minimize all applications except the one you want to optimize, and
use Task Manager to Tile the application.

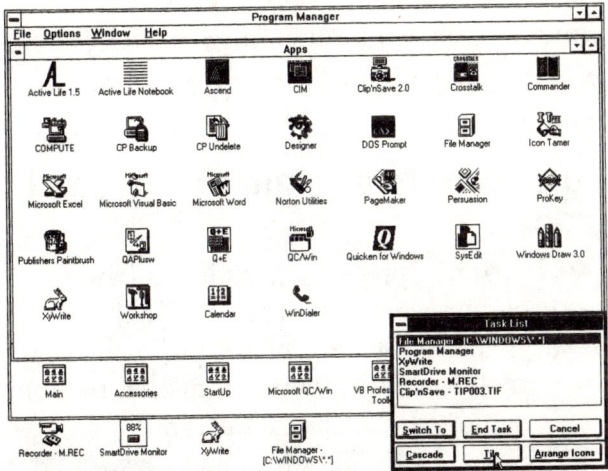

*To optimize Program Manager's size, call Task
Manager and click on Tile.*

Arrange all icons— program item icons, document icons, and application icons

Icons are both the joy and the curse of Windows. Using Windows' three types of icons will only help you if the icons are arranged in an organized and orderly way.

Learn how to arrange each type of icon.

- To arrange program item icons (the Program Manager icons on which you double-click to run programs), select one and choose Window, Arrange Icons from Program Manager's menu bar.

- To arrange document icons (minimized Program Manager groups), select one and choose Window, Arrange Icons from Program Manager's menu bar.

- To arrange application icons (programs that are running but minimized on the desktop), select one, call Task Manager, and click on Arrange Icons or press Alt-A.

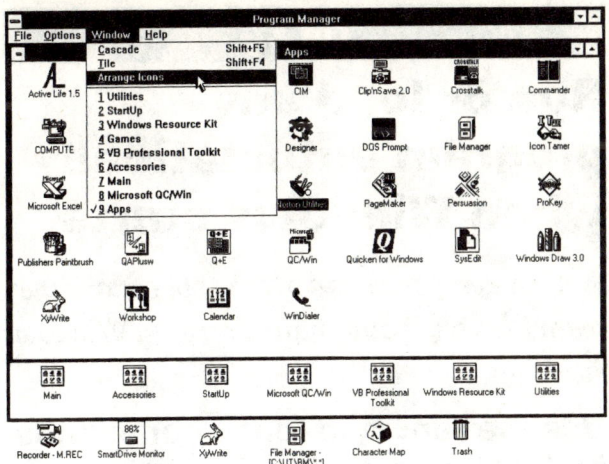

Choose Window, Arrange Icons to arrange program item icons and document icons. Call Task Manager, and click on Arrange Icons to arrange application icons.

Run or load any program automatically when Windows starts

Almost everyone has certain applications they want to execute automatically when Windows starts up.

Use the run= and load= commands in WIN.INI or the Startup group.

Let's say that you want to run Calculator and Write every time Windows boots up. You want Calculator to be the active application, and you want Write to be minimized.

- To run an application—that is, to make it the active program—place its name after run= in WIN.INI. To run Calculator, you'd use the line run=calculator.exe.

- To load an application—that is, to run it minimized on the desktop—place its name after load= in WIN.INI. To load Write, you'd use the line load=write.exe.

You can put several applications in each line, separated by a space, up to 127 characters total. If the program is on your path (which both Calculator and Write are), you only need to specify the filename. If the program is not on your path, however, specify the complete path to the program.

The method above works for both Windows

3.0 and 3.1, but 3.1 has a new Program Manager group called Startup that holds the icons of the programs you want to run automatically when Windows starts. Here's how to use it:

● To run a program with Windows 3.1, drag the program's icon from any group to Startup, and choose File, Properties, and make sure Run Minimized *is not* checked.

● To load a program with Windows 3.1, drag the program's icon from any group to Startup, and choose File, Properties, and make sure Run Minimized *is* checked.

With Windows 3.1, you can prevent the programs in your Startup group from running by holding down the Shift key while Windows boots. The Shift key doesn't affect programs specified in your load= and run= lines, however—they will load and run normally.

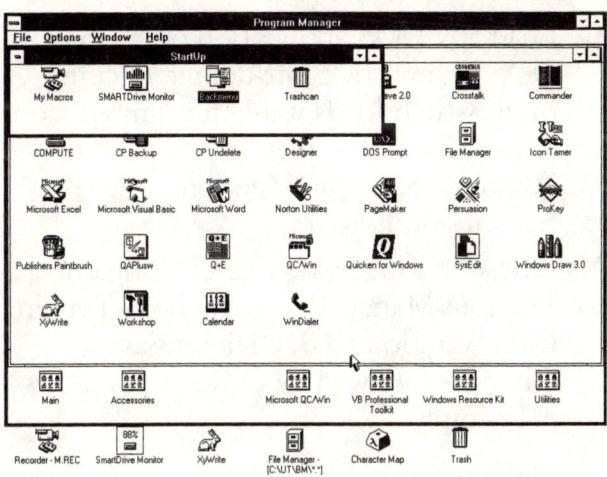

To automatically run or load a program, add the program to your Startup group, or the run= or load= line in WIN.INI.

Save your configuration without quitting Windows

When you've arranged Program Manager's main window, document windows, icons, and document icons just the way you want them, you'll want to save your setup. However, Windows only saves your setup when you exit.

Fool Windows into saving your changes.

Windows 3.1

❶ Hold down the Shift key.

❷ Select File, Exit (using either a mouse or the keyboard). Windows will save your configuration but won't close.

Windows 3.0 or 3.1

❶ Load any DOS application other than DOS Prompt by Shift-double-clicking on it, which loads it as a minimized icon rather than full screen. If you're using Windows 3.1, select Options, Save Settings on Exit.

❷ Exit Windows by double-clicking on Program Manager's control box. If you're using Windows 3.0, click on Save Changes followed by OK. For Windows 3.1, simply click on OK.

❸ You'll see the message "Application still active; exit the application and then try closing Windows."

❹ Click on OK. Your setup has been saved, but you're still in Windows.

When you exit Windows, the first thing it does is save your setup. Next, it automatically closes all Windows applications, giving each a chance to prompt you to save changes, if there are any. Windows doesn't have this control over DOS applications, so it aborts the exit and asks you to manually close each program. Windows 3.1, however, will exit if DOS Prompt is still active, so it's wise to choose another DOS application to stop Windows' exit.

Install any icon on Program Manager

Almost all Windows applications come with icons embedded in their executable (EXE) files, but what do you do about icons for DOS programs?

Use icons from other Windows programs.

❶ Select the DOS Prompt from the Main group.

❷ Choose File, Properties, Change Icon.

❸ In the File Name text box, type in C:\WINDOWS\PROGRAM.EXE, if it isn't already there.

❹ Click on the scroll bar (or the View Next button for Windows 3.0) until you've found an icon you like.

Windows 3.1 comes with a special file, MORICONS.DLL, that contains icons for many popular DOS programs. You also can find icons in other Windows EXE files, some DLLs, and ICOs, which are individual icon files.

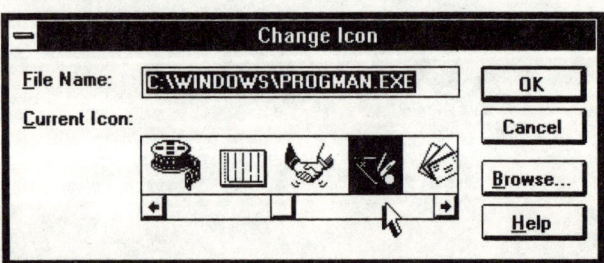

Click on the scroll bar to see all the icons available in PROGMAN.EXE.

Bypass Task Manager and zoom between Windows and DOS programs

You can use the Task Manager or press Alt-Esc to move between Windows and DOS applications, but both methods can be slow.

Use Alt-Tab and Alt-Shift-Tab.

❶ Run any DOS application. (If you don't have one handy, run DOS Prompt from the Main group.)

❷ With the DOS application full screen, press Alt-Tab to cycle forward through all the applications on your desktop. You'll see the name of the application displayed on a band at the top of your screen.

❸ Press Alt-Shift-Tab to cycle backward through your applications.

Fly between windowed and full screen DOS applications

You can press Alt-Space and use the menus to change a DOS application from windowed to full screen, but it's an awkward process.

Use Alt-Enter to toggle between any DOS program's full-screen and windowed states.

❶ Run any DOS application, either windowed or full screen.

❷ Press Alt-Enter to change the application to its other state—full screen if it's currently windowed, windowed if it's currently full screen.

Maximize and restore windows without using buttons

All windows have minimize and maximize or restore buttons, but they're small and difficult to click on, especially if you're in a hurry.

Double-click on the title bar.

● Double-click anywhere on the title bar to maximize a restored window.

● Double-click anywhere on the title bar to restore a maximized window.

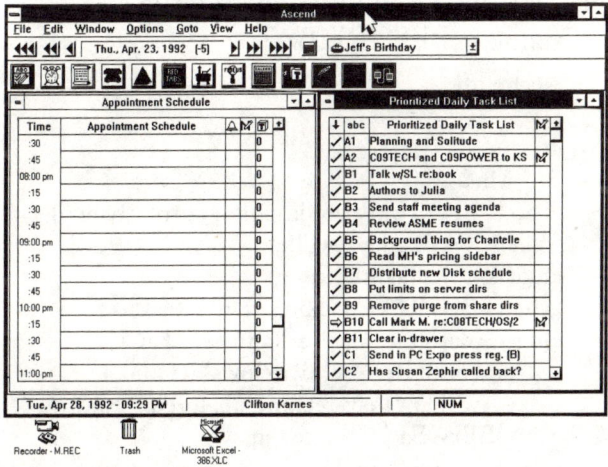

To maximize a restored window, double-click on the title bar.

Uninstall any Windows program

Almost every Windows program installs a large number of files—often in several directories. In addition, most programs make changes to your AUTOEXEC.BAT, CONFIG.SYS, WIN.INI, or SYSTEM.INI, and sometimes all four. Keeping track of the files and changes associated with an application is nearly impossible.

Use BEFORE and AFTER.

❶ Type in the following batch file and name it BEFORE.BAT:

```
@echo off
cls
c:
cd \windows
echo [BEFORE] Recording files currently on disk
    (this will take a while)...
chkdsk/v >c:snapshot.tmp
echo [BEFORE] Checking system files...
copy c:snapshot.tmp + c:\autoexec.bat +
    c:\config.sys + c:\windows\win.ini +
    c:\windows\system.ini c:before.txt >nul
echo [BEFORE] Cleaning up...
erase c:snapshot.tmp
cd \
```

❷ Type in the following batch file and call it AFTER.BAT:

```
@echo off
if "%1" == "" goto end
cls
c:
cd \windows
echo [AFTER] Recording files currently on disk
    (this will take a while)...
chkdsk/v >c:snapshot.tmp
echo [AFTER] Checking system files...
copy c:snapshot.tmp + c:\autoexec.bat +
    c:\config.sys + c:\windows\win.ini +
    c:\windows\system.ini c:after.txt >nul
erase c:snapshot.tmp
echo [AFTER] Checking for changes...
fc c:before.txt c:after.txt >c:%1
type %1 | more
goto stop
:end
echo Please specify a filename for the changes
:stop
```

❸ Before you install any program (Windows or DOS, for that matter) run BEFORE.BAT. It will take a snapshot of every file on your disk as well as the contents of your AUTOEXEC.BAT, CONFIG.SYS, WIN.INI, and SYSTEM.INI files.

❹ After you install a program, run AFTER.BAT, by typing AFTER *filename*, at the DOS prompt. *Filename* will contain a record of every file added (or deleted) by the installation program and any changes made to your system files.

❺ Save this and all other files with this installation information in a subdirectory for future reference.

Replace Program Manager with another shell

Program Manager is Windows' default shell, but you might prefer to use a different shell, one that takes less memory, for example.

Change the shell= line in SYSTEM.INI.

❶ Run SysEdit and select your SYSTEM.INI file.

❷ Find the line that says

shell=progman.exe

❸ Change the line to

shell=winfile.exe.

❹ Experiment with other programs. The MS-DOS Executive (MSDOS.EXE), for example, makes an excellent shell.

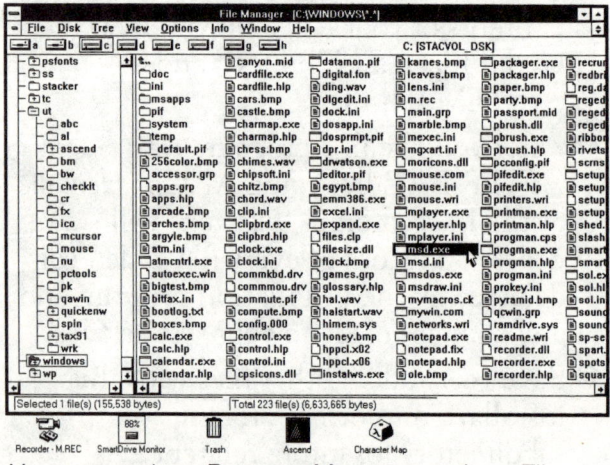

You can replace Program Manager and run File Manager as your default shell.

Install documents as icons

It's often more convenient to organize your Program Manager groups in terms of documents rather than applications.

Install associated documents on program groups.

Install a text file document as an icon.

❶ In Program Manager, make the Accessories group active, and choose File, New, Program Item.

❷ In Description, type Winini.

❸ In Command Line, type WININI.WRI (or WININI.TXT for Windows 3.0).

❹ When you click on this icon, you'll run Write, which will load the associated WRI file (or you'll run Notepad for Windows 3.0).

❺ If you want to change the icon, select File, Properties, Change Icon, and type the name of an ICO file, or an EXE or DLL that contains icons.

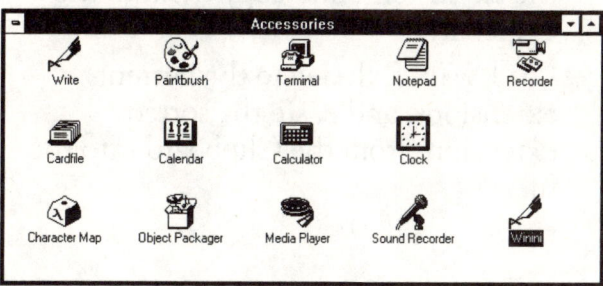

You can install any document as an icon on a Program Manager group.

Sort the extension list in your WIN.INI file

The extension list in your WIN.INI file grows large very quickly and is difficult to maintain.

Sort the list. Use a word processor with a sort block command or cut the section from WIN.INI, put the text in a separate file, and sort the file using the DOS SORT command.

❶ Run Notepad and call WIN.INI.

❷ Find the [Extensions] section.

❸ Select all the extensions and copy them to the Clipboard.

❹ Open a new Notepad file and paste the extensions into it.

❺ Save the file with the name EXT.TXT.

❻ Run DOS Prompt, and type SORT <EXT.TXT>EXT2.TXT

❼ Delete EXT.TXT.

❽ Load EXT2.TXT into Notepad, select the extensions, and copy them to the Clipboard.

❾ Load WIN.INI, delete the current extensions, and paste the sorted extensions from the Clipboard into the file.

❿ When a program adds associations to this list, it will add them at the bottom. Every now and then, edit this file and put the entries at the bottom in alphabetical order.

Avoid opening a large number of groups

If you have all your frequently used applications stored in a large number of Program Manager groups, you may find yourself wasting a lot of time opening, closing, and rearranging group windows to find your applications.

Put the programs you use regularly on one group.

❶ Create a group called Apps (or any other name you choose) and minimize it.

❷ Open each of your other groups and drag the icon of every program you use regularly to Apps.

❸ Minimize all groups except Apps, and choose Window, Tile.

❹ Save your configuration.

It's worth noting that with Windows 3.0, each time you display a new group, its icons take precious system resources that Windows can never reclaim. Windows 3.1 handles icons in a different way, so they don't use system resources.

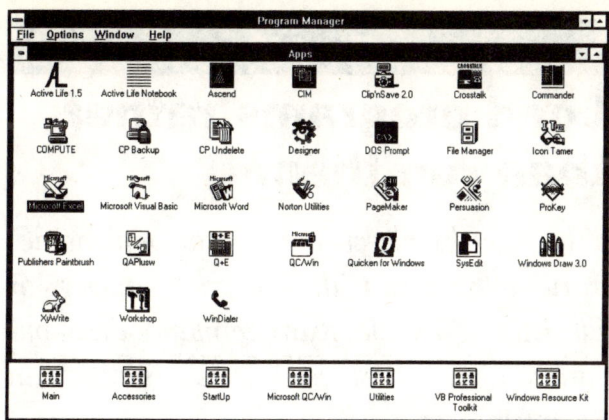

To avoid opening a large number of groups, place all the programs you use frequently on a single group.

Load programs rather than run them

When you double-click on an icon or filename, or run a program with Program Manager's or File Manager's File, Run command, the application runs full screen, which is often an inconvenience.

Load programs you want to run minimized.

● Shift-double-click on any icon in Program Manager or any filename in File Manager or MS-DOS Executive that you want to run minimized.

Don't let Recorder record your mouse clicks

If Recorder records your mouse clicks, any mouse movements you make will only be played back correctly when the position and configuration of your Windows is exactly the same as when the macro was recorded.

Tell Recorder to only record your keystrokes.

❶ Select Options, Preferences.

❷ In the Record Mouse drop-down list box, select Ignore Mouse.

❸ Press OK.

Create a macro to view or edit nonassociated text files

With File Manager, there are two ways you can view files easily: You can associate the file's extension with Notepad (or another text editing program) and double-click on the file, or you can drag the file to a Notepad icon (in Windows 3.1). The first method only works if the file is associated, and the second method requires that Notepad be minimized on your desktop.

Use a Recorder macro to load the file at the cursor in File Manager (or MS-DOS Executive) into Notepad.

❶ In File Manager or MS-DOS Executive, Select a file to load into Notepad.

❷ Open Recorder, configure the program to ignore mouse movement, choose a name for your macro, and start recording.

❸ In File Manager, press Alt-F, P, and Ctrl-Insert to copy the selected filename to the Clipboard. Press Tab, Tab, Enter to exit the dialog box.

❹ Press Alt-F, R, and type NOTEPAD.EXE in the text box followed by a space.

❺ Press Shift-Insert to paste the name of the file into the text box.

❻ Press Enter.

❼ Stop Recording the macro, and assign the macro a keypress such as Ctrl-Alt-N.

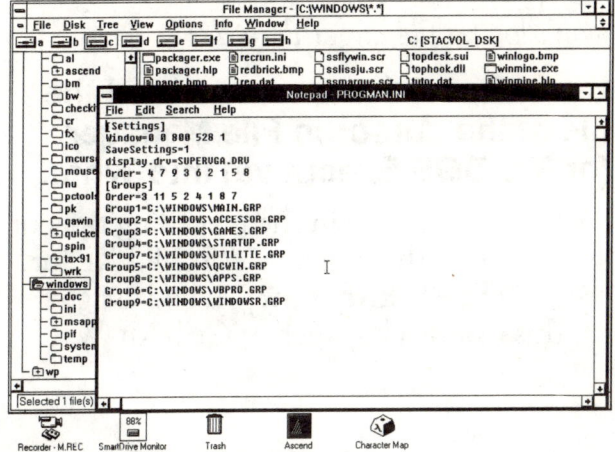

Create a Recorder macro to load files into Notepad with a single key combination.

Create a macro to view or edit any file

Notepad is great for viewing small files, but it won't load a file larger than 57K.

Use a Recorder macro to load the file at the cursor in File Manager (or MS-DOS Executive) into Write.

● Follow the steps in the preceding tip, but substitute the program WRITE.EXE for NOTEPAD.EXE in step 4, and assign this macro a key such as Ctrl-Alt-W.

Add search and replace to Notepad

Notepad doesn't offer a search and replace function.

Simulate search and replace with a few repeated keystrokes.

❶ Select Search, Find, and type in the string for which you wish to search.

❷ At the first search hit, type in the replacement string, select it, and copy it to the Clipboard.

❸ Press F3, Shift-Insert repeatedly to find the next matching text string and replace it.

If you use this search and replace simulation often, you may want to put the F3, Shift-Insert key sequence in a Recorder macro to automate the replacement process.

Create a macro to display a wildcard listing

To view files by extension type in File Manager, you have to go through slow menus and dialog boxes.

Use a Recorder macro to automatically display all files with the same extension as the file at the cursor.

❶ Place the cursor on any filename in File Manager that ends with a three-character extension.

❷ Run Recorder and prepare to record a macro.

❸ Press Alt-F, P, and press cursor left five times.

❹ Press Shift-Home to define the part of the filename before the extension.

❺ Press Delete.

❻ Press *.

❼ Press Home, followed by Shift-End to define the wildcard filename.

❽ Press Ctrl-Insert to copy the wildcard to the Clipboard. Press Tab, Tab, Enter to exit the dialog box.

❾ Press Alt-V, T (C for Windows 3.0), and Shift-Insert to paste the wildcard into the text box.

❿ Press Enter to display files with the wildcard, then stop recording.

This macro works for files with one-, two-, or three-character extensions, but will not work for files with no extension.

Use the typographic symbols for quotes and dashes in Write and other Windows applications

Polished documents demand special typographic symbols for single quotes, double quotes, em dashes, and en dashes.

Use Windows extended ANSI character set.

● To produce beginning and ending single quotation marks, make sure Num Lock is on, and press Alt-0145 and Alt-0146 on the numeric keypad.

● To produce beginning and ending double quotation marks, make sure Num Lock is on, and press Alt-0147 and Alt-0148 on the numeric keypad.

● To produce an em dash (often crudely represented by two hyphens --), make sure Num Lock is on, and press Alt-0151 on the numeric keypad.

● To produce an en dash (the typographic symbol that's longer than a hyphen but shorter than an em dash and is used to indicate ranges), make sure Num Lock is on, and press Alt-0150 on the numeric keypad.

Unfortunately, you can't use Recorder to save these keystrokes in a macro. This is a Recorder bug.

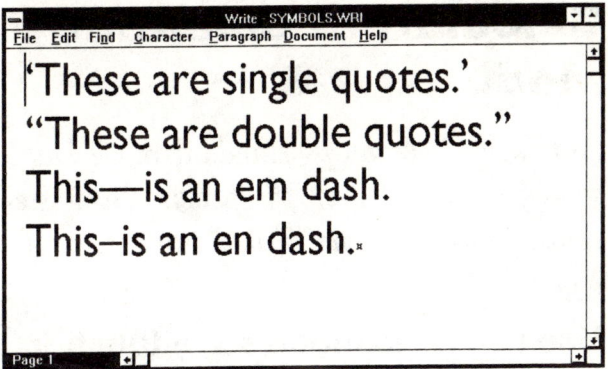

Use Windows' extended ANSI character set to create typographic symbols.

Figure square roots in Calculator's scientific mode

Although Calculator's standard mode has a square root key (sqrt), this function is mysteriously missing from Calculator's scientific mode.

Use scientific mode's x^y function to figure square roots.

❶ To find the square root of any number, type in the number.

❷ Press the x^y key.

❸ Type 0.5, and press =.

Get Cardfile to dial the phone number instead of the ZIP code

Cardfile dials the first number it finds, whether this is a phone number or not.

Make sure the first number Cardfile finds is the phone number.

● Put the phone number on the card index line immediately following the index entry.

Move and copy files with File Manager

When you drag a file from one place to another in File Manager, it sometimes copies the file and it sometimes moves it.

Learn File Manager's defaults and how to override them.

- To copy a file from one drive to another, simply drag the filename. When files are dragged between drives, the default is to copy them.

- To move a file from one drive to another, press the Alt key and drag the file. Pressing the Alt key overrides the default.

- To move a file from one subdirectory to another, drag it. When files are dragged between subdirectories on the same drive, the default is to move them.

- To copy a file from one subdirectory to another, press the Ctrl key and drag the file. Pressing the Ctrl key overrides the default.

Cut and paste subdirectories with File Manager

To really keep your directory tree organized, you need to be able to move subdirectories from one place to another.

Drag subdirectories from one place to another in File Manager.

❶ In the directory tree in File Manager, click on any subdirectory you want to move.

❷ Drag the subdirectory to the destination directory.

Windows 3.0 displays messages indicating that only the files in the subdirectory are being copied to the destination subdirectory, but in fact, the entire subdirectory is being moved. Windows 3.1's messages are accurate and more reassuring.

Capture a Windows screen

Almost everyone at one time or another needs to capture Windows or DOS screens.

Use Windows' built-in screen-capture.

- To capture the entire Windows desktop, press Print Screen.

- To capture just the active Window, press Alt-Print Screen.

- To capture a DOS application, press Alt-Print Screen. If the application is full screen, the information will be captured as text. If the application is windowed, the screen will be captured as a graphic.

Master Windows' Clipboard

If you're not using Windows' Clipboard, you're working too hard.

Learn the four keystrokes that control Windows' Clipboard.

❶ To copy to the Clipboard, press Ctrl-Insert. When you copy to the Clipboard, your original selection is left untouched.

❷ To cut to the Clipboard, press Shift-Delete. When you cut to the Clipboard, your original selection is deleted.

❸ To paste from the Clipboard, press Shift-Insert. When you paste from the Clipboard, the selection stored in the Clipboard stays there.

❹ To cut the selection without sending it to the Clipboard, press Delete.

Paste a screen into Paintbrush

When you paste an image of your entire desktop into Paintbrush, it clips the image.

Use Paintbrush's Zoom Out command before pasting.

❶ Capture your screen with Print Screen.

❷ Run Paintbrush.

❸ Select Options, Image Attribute, Default, and OK.

❹ Select View, Zoom Out.

❺ Select Edit, Paste. If the screen doesn't appear, select Edit and Paste again (this is a bug).

❻ Select View, View Picture to verify the entire image has been pasted. (Click a mouse button, or press any key to exit View Picture.)

❼ Select View, Zoom In.

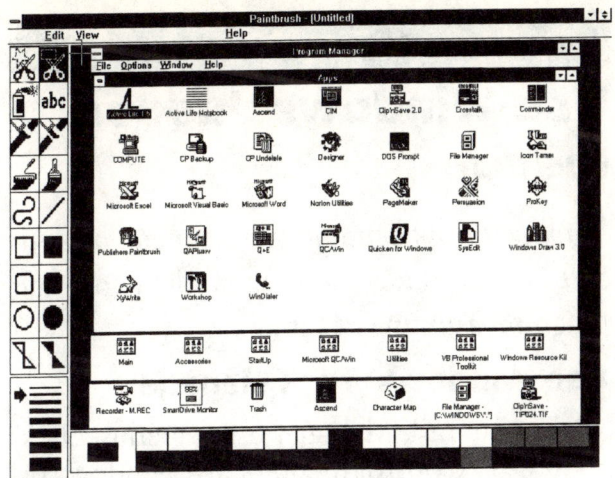

With a little preparation, you can paste a screen of your entire desktop into Paintbrush without clipping it.

Use Windows' hidden menu.

Finding the application you want can be difficult if you have more than three or four programs running at a time.

Use Windows' Task Manager.

❶ To call Task Manager using menus, click on the Control menu of any window (or press Alt-Space) and select Switch To.

❷ To call Task Manager using the mouse, simply double-click on any open space on the desktop.

❸ To call Task Manager using the keyboard, press Ctrl-Esc.

❹ After calling Task Manager, double-click on any application displayed in the list box to switch to that application. With the keyboard, you can either use cursor keys to move through applications or press the first letter of an application's name to select it and hit Enter to switch.

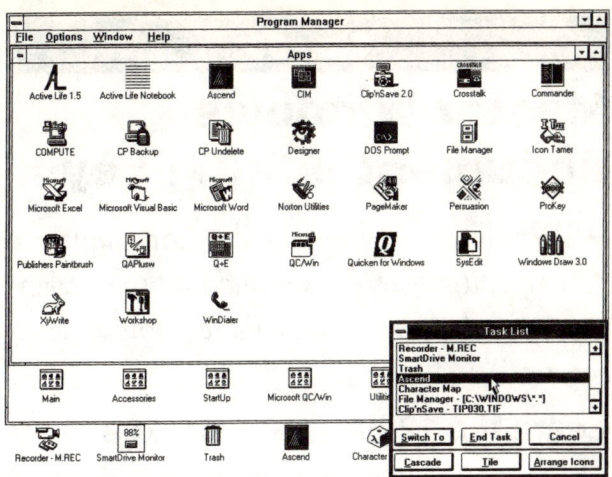

Move between the programs on your desktop with Task Manager.

Master Windows document editing keys

All Windows text-based applications support a core of editing keystrokes and mouse conventions. Unless you learn these, you'll never master Windows.

Learn the 12 basic keystrokes.

- *Right*, *Left*, *Up*, and *Down* move the cursor one character in the direction of the key pressed.

- *Home* moves to the beginning of the current line.

- *End* moves to the end of the current line.

- *Ctrl-Right* moves one word to the right.

- *Ctrl-Left* moves one word to the left.

- *Ctrl-Home* moves to the beginning of the document.

- *Ctrl-End* moves to the end of the document.

- *Shift-Right* and *Shift-Left* define text one character to the right or left.

- *Shift-Up* and *Shift-Down* define text one line up or down.

- *Shift-Home* defines text to the beginning of the line.

- *Shift-End* defines text to the end of the line.
- *Alt-Backspace* undoes the last edit (not all Windows applications support this key combination).

Manipulating selected text with the Clipboard is discussed in Tip #30.

Use Terminal's function key buttons

Most telecommunications sessions involve typing the same keystrokes over and over in response to online prompts.

Install Terminal's function key buttons so you can click your responses.

❶ In Terminal, select Settings, Function Keys.

❷ In the Key Name text box, put the name you want to appear on the button. For the first key, type Enter.

❸ In the Command text box, type the keystrokes you want to be executed when you click on the button (or press the appropriate function key). For the Enter key, put ^M. The caret (^) indicates that this is a control key, and the M is the control code for Enter.

❹ Since most BBSs allow you to sign off by typing a G (for goodbye) followed by Enter, for the second key, type Goodbye in the Key Name text box and g^M in the Command text box.

❺ Fill in the other buttons with the most common menu choices you find on your online service.

❻ Check Keys Visible when you've finished, and click on OK.

❼ Save your settings with File, Save before you exit.

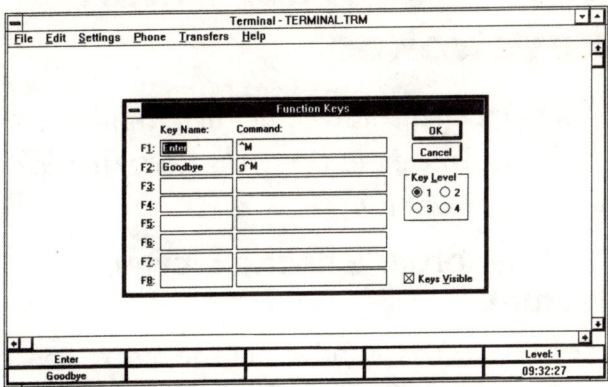

Terminal's function key buttons make telecommunicating as easy as clicking with your mouse.

View Recorder macro keystrokes

After you create a Recorder macro, it's often essential to review its keystrokes to see if it does what you want it to.

Use Recorder's secret viewer feature.

❶ Run Recorder and select the macro you want to view.

❷ Hold down the Shift key and select Macro, Properties (either with a mouse or the keyboard).

❸ Your macro's keypresses will appear in a list box.

Reading this keystroke list can be tricky. You'll see two entries for each keypress—one for when the key was pressed and one for when the key was released. For example, if you press the A key, you'll see Key Down, a; Key Up, a. Shift, Alt, and Ctrl keys also have up and down states so a key combination with one of these will have four entries in the list. For example, Shift-A will look like this:

> Key Down, Shift
> Key Down, a
> Key Up, a
> Key Up, Shift

Note that shifted characters don't appear in the listing as we see them on screen. For example, the asterisk (*), which is the shifted state of the 8 key, is listed like this:

Key Down, Shift
Key Down, 8
Key Up, 8
Key Up, Shift

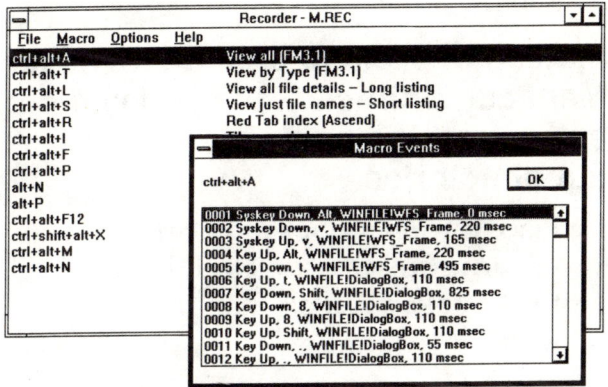

Hold down the Shift key and select Macros, Properties to see a listing of a macro's keystrokes.

Display a full tree with File Manager

When you select a drive in File Manager, the tree window displays the first level of subdirectories only.

Instead of clicking on a drive in File Manager, Shift-click to display the entire tree, including all subdirectories.

● Place the mouse cursor over the icon of the drive you wish to select, hold down the Shift key, and click on the drive icon.

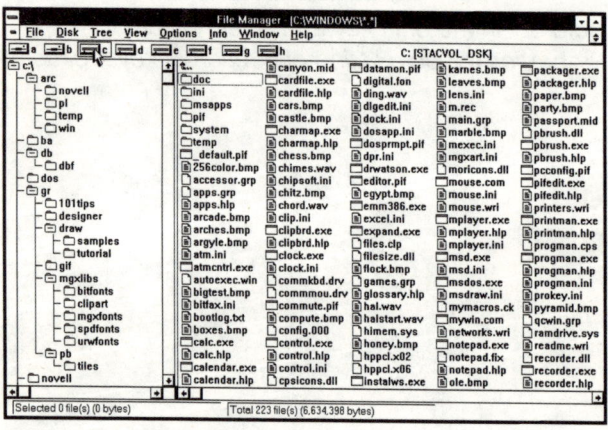

Shift-click on a drive icon to display the drive's full tree.

Teach Recorder to close itself

Since multiple Recorder sessions aren't allowed in Windows, it's often essential to have a Recorder macro close Recorder, but it's impossible for Recorder to record a macro that kills itself (doubtlessly in the spirit of self preservation).

Fool Recorder by using an alias and closing the alias.

❶ If you have Windows 3.0, run Reversi; if you're using 3.1, run RegEdit.

❷ Run Recorder and record your macro.

❸ When it's time to close Recorder, press Ctrl-Esc to bring up Task Manager.

❹ Press R to move the selection to Reversi or RegEdit.

❺ Press Alt-E to end the task.

❻ Now run your macro. When the Recorder macro presses R in Task Manager it will find itself and terminate (as long as you're not running another Windows program that starts with R).

Open two drive windows in File Manager

Copying files from one drive to another in File Manager is difficult unless you open two drive windows simultaneously.

With one drive window already open, Shift-double-click on any other drive window.

❶ Open the first drive window by clicking (or Shift-clicking) on the drive icon.

❷ Open the second drive window by Shift-double-clicking on the drive icon.

❸ Choose Window, Tile or press Shift-F4 to arrange the windows.

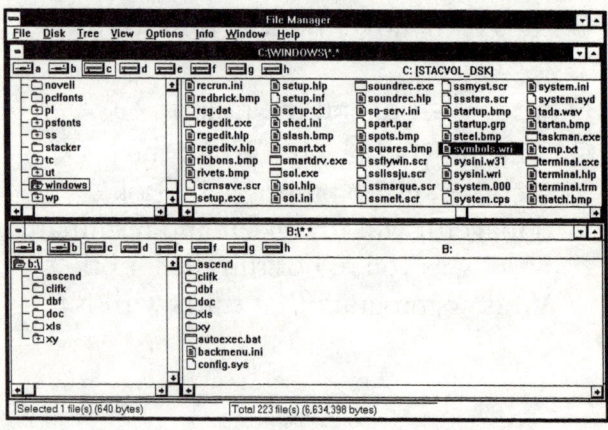

Shift-double-click on a drive icon to open an additional drive window.

Double-time your printer

Windows' Print Manager lets you multitask while you're printing, but it slows down printing considerably.

Tell Windows not to use Print Manager.

❶ Run Control Panel, found on the Main group.

❷ Double-click on the Printers icon.

❸ Uncheck the Use Print Manager box.

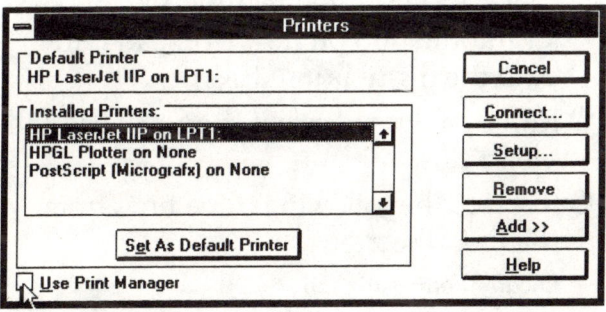

Uncheck Use Print Manager to send your print jobs directly to the printer.

Decrease the size of your Windows system screen fonts

If you're using a VGA display, Windows default system font may be too large for your tastes.

Replace the default VGA font with Windows' EGA font.

❶ Install the files EGASYS.FON, EGAOEM.FON, and EGAFIX.FON from the Windows distribution disks into your SYSTEM subdirectory (see Tip #68 for information on how to expand files from the distribution disks).

❷ Run SysEdit and select the SYSTEM.INI file to edit.

❸ Replace the following three lines from the [boot] section

fixedfon.fon=vgafix.fon
oemfonts.fon=vgaoem.fon
fonts.fon=vgasys.fon

with

fixedfon.fon=egafix.fon
oemfonts.fon=egaoem.fon
fonts.fon=egasys.fon

❹ Reboot Windows.

Here's how Windows' three display fonts compare on a VGA system in 800 × 600 mode:

Display	Font Lines in maximized Notepad
VGAFON.FON	36
EGAFON.FON	54
8514FON.FON	27

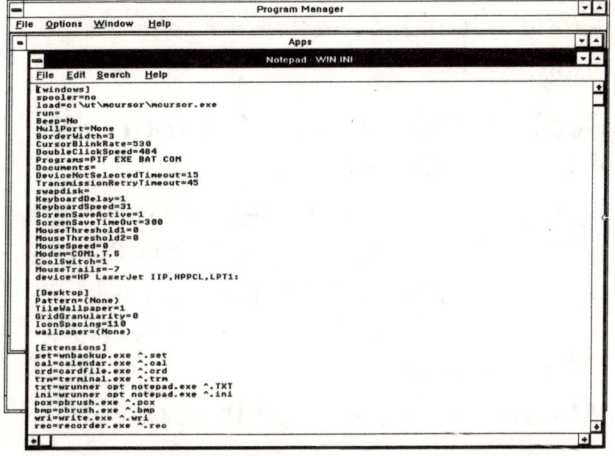

Install Windows' EGA fonts to make your system type smaller and display more information on the screen.

Increase the size of your Windows system screen fonts

If you're using a VGA display, Windows default system font may be too small for your tastes.

Replace the default VGA font with Windows 8514 font.

❶ Install the files 8514OEM.FON, 8514SYS.FON, and 8514FIX.FON from the Windows distribution disks (see Tip #68 for information on how to expand files from the distribution disks).

❷ Run SysEdit and select the SYSTEM.INI file to edit.

❸ Replace the following three lines from the [boot] section

fixedfon.fon=vgafix.fon
oemfonts.fon=vgaoem.fon
fonts.fon=vgasys.fon

with

fixedfon.fon=8514fixfon
oemfonts.fon=8514oem.fon
fonts.fon=8514sys.fon

❹ Reboot Windows.

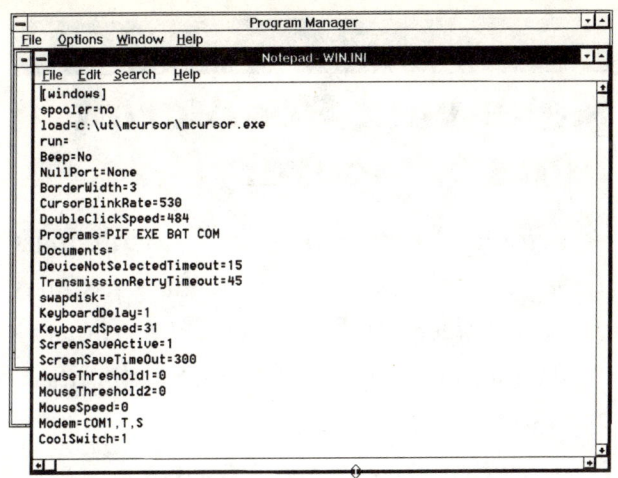

```
                          Program Manager                    ▼ ▲
 File   Options   Window   Help
 ▼ ─                      Notepad - WIN.INI                   ▼ ▲
  File   Edit   Search   Help
 [windows]                                                       ▲
 spooler=no
 load=c:\ut\mcursor\mcursor.exe
 run=
 Beep=No
 NullPort=None
 BorderWidth=3
 CursorBlinkRate=530
 DoubleClickSpeed=484
 Programs=PIF EXE BAT COM
 Documents=
 DeviceNotSelectedTimeout=15
 TransmissionRetryTimeout=45
 swapdisk=
 KeyboardDelay=1
 KeyboardSpeed=31
 ScreenSaveActive=1
 ScreenSaveTimeOut=300
 MouseThreshold1=0
 MouseThreshold2=0
 MouseSpeed=0
 Modem=COM1,T,S
 CoolSwitch=1                                                    ▼
 ◄ │                          ◊                               │ ►
```

Install Windows' 8514 fonts to make your system type larger and easier to read.

Make your PostScript fonts temporary

By default, Windows installs PostScript fonts as permanent, which means that it assumes they are resident in the printer. Often, however, it's more convenient to download fonts at print time.

Make your PostScript fonts temporary.

❶ Run SysEdit and select WIN.INI.

❷ Find the [PostScript] section.

❸ Each line will indicate the full path to the font's PFM file. Add a comma and the complete path to the PFB file to each line. For example, change

c:\psfonts\pfm\aachen.pfm

to

c:\psfonts\pfm\aachen.pfm,c:\psfonts\aachen.pfb

Use Windows' extended character set

The standard character set is fine for most applications, but if you need fractions, typographical symbols, or accented characters, you're out of luck.

Use Windows extended ANSI character set.

❶ To find out which characters are available in the extended ANSI character set, look at the chart in Appendix B of the Windows 3.0 manual or run the Windows 3.1 utility Character Map, found on the Accessories group.

❷ To use Character Map, select your character by double-clicking on it. Then press Copy to send the character to the Clipboard. To use the numeric keypad, make sure the Num Lock key is on, and type Alt-0 followed by the number of the character.

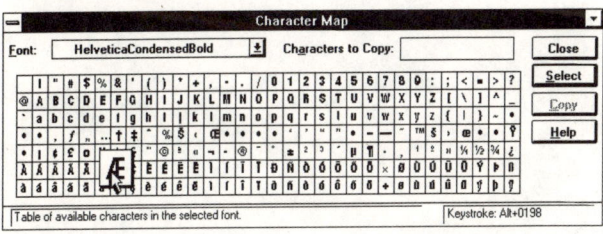

Run Character Map to see the extended ANSI characters and the keystroke combinations required to access them.

Multitask DOS apps on the fly

After you've used the PIF editor to configure a DOS application so it doesn't run in the background, you may occasionally need to allow the program to multitask temporarily.

Use the Settings option on the Control menu to change the program's operation to Background.

❶ If the application isn't running in a window, press Alt-Enter.

❷ Select the Control menu in the upper left corner of the window with the mouse, or press Alt-Space bar.

❸ Choose Settings, click on Background, and OK.

Try setting the DOS Prompt (found on the Main group) to background operation and use its multitasking ability to format disks in the background while you work in another window.

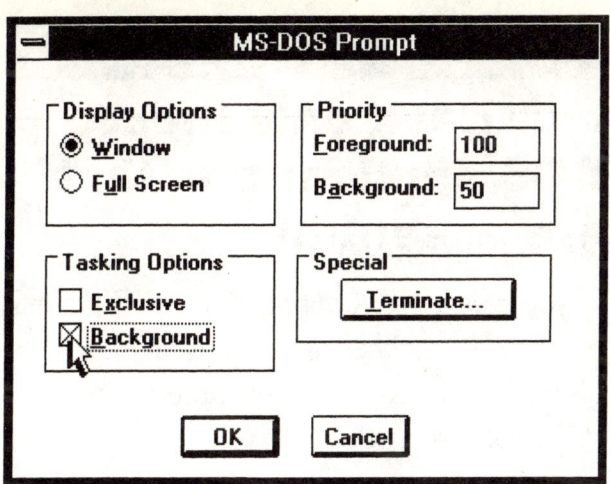

To multitask DOS applications on the fly, call the Control menu, choose Settings, and click on Background.

Multitask only those DOS applications that are essential

If you edit a DOS application's PIF file and mark it as capable of running in the background, Windows will slow down every time that application runs.

Allow only those programs that *must* run in the background—such as telecommunications programs—to run in the background.

❶ Load each DOS program's PIF file.

❷ In the Execution section, make sure that neither Background nor Exclusive is checked, unless it's essential that the program run in the background.

Terminate a DOS application that's crashed

When a DOS application crashes, it's impossible to terminate it normally.

Use Settings on the Control menu, or, if you have Windows 3.1, press Ctrl-Alt-Delete.

For either Windows 3.0 or 3.1:

❶ Minimize the application by pressing Alt-Esc.

❷ Click on the application once to bring up its Control menu and select Settings.

❸ Click on Terminate and OK in the following dialog box.

For Windows 3.1:

❶ With the DOS application either full screen or windowed, press Ctrl-Alt-Delete.

❷ At the next screen, press Enter.

Use hotkeys for DOS applications

Moving between DOS applications can be tedious. Using Task Manager helps, but it doesn't really streamline your switching.

Set up a hotkey for each DOS application in the PIF editor.

❶ Run the PIF editor, load the PIF for any DOS application you use frequently, and click on the Advanced button.

❷ At the bottom of the screen, beside Application Shortcut Key, type in a shortcut key for the program. Although most key combinations will work, some will interfere with other applications' key combinations. One suggestion is to use Ctrl-Alt followed by the key you wish to use. For example, you could have the DOS Prompt set to use the hotkey Ctrl-Alt-D.

Windows 3.1 lets you assign hotkeys to Windows applications, too. To use this feature, simply select the icon of the program, then choose File, Properties, and under Shortcut Key, type the keystrokes for your hotkey.

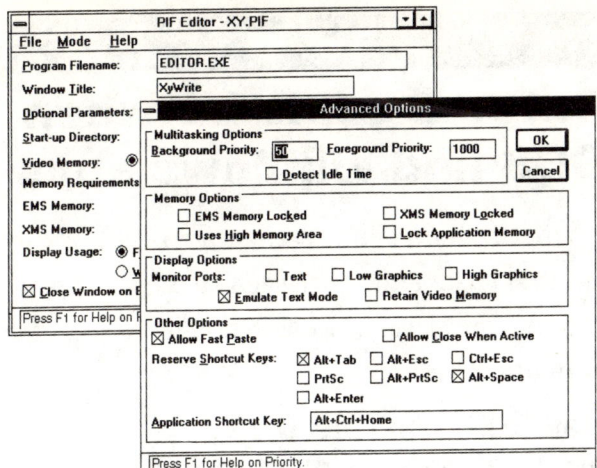

Use the PIF Editor to assign a hotkey to your DOS applications.

Cut and paste between DOS and Windows apps

There are many times when it's necessary to cut and paste either between two DOS applications or between a DOS application and a Windows one.

Use Edit from the DOS application's Control menu.

❶ To copy text from a DOS application, run the application in a window (press Alt-Enter if it isn't running in a window already).

❷ Select the Control menu in the upper left corner of the window with the mouse, or press Alt-Space bar.

❸ Select Edit, Mark.

❹ Click and drag the mouse to select the text you want to copy.

❺ Press Enter or choose Edit, Copy from the Control menu. Now your text is in the Clipboard.

❻ If you want to unselect text without copying it to the Clipboard, press Esc.

❼ To paste, make sure the application is windowed and the cursor is at the correct location, then select Edit, Paste from the Control menu.

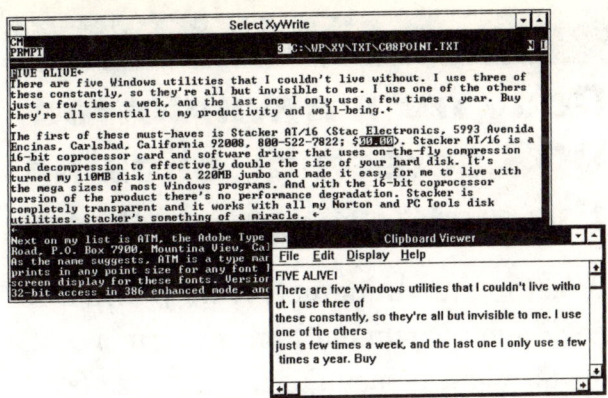

To copy text from a DOS app to the Clipboard, window the app, select Edit, Mark from the Control menu, and click and drag the mouse to select the block to copy.

Copy from a windowed DOS screen by clicking the right mouse button

When you're cutting and pasting from a DOS application, continually pressing Enter or using the Control menu to copy selected text to the Clipboard will slow you down.

Use the right mouse button to copy text to the Clipboard.

❶ Follow steps 1 through 4 in the preceding tip.

❷ Instead of pressing Enter or using the Control menu, simply click the right mouse button to copy text to the Clipboard.

Start each Windows DOS session with a special prompt

If you run programs from Windows and from DOS, it's sometimes difficult to remember whether you're at the DOS prompt itself or a DOS prompt in Windows.

When you run the DOS Prompt from Windows, set the PROMPT environmental variable so the session is identified as a DOS session in Windows.

❶ Run Notepad and start a new file called DOS.BAT.

❷ Type in the following lines, substituting anything you'd like for [WIN]:

PROMPT [WIN] PG
COMMAND

❸ Use this batch file as your DOS prompt from Windows, and it will look like this:
[WIN] C:\>

Exit Windows even when a DOS application is running

Normally, you can't exit Windows when a DOS application is running.

Create a PIF file for the application that allows fast exit.

❶ Open the DOS program's PIF file, or create a PIF and fill in the basic parameters.

❷ Click on the Advanced button and check the box Allow Close When Active.

To allow Windows to exit even when a DOS application is running, check Allow Close When Active in the Advanced section of the application's PIF file.

Speed up DOS programs by fine tuning SYSTEM.INI

The wrong settings in the 386 enhanced mode section of your SYSTEM.INI file can slow Windows down.

Edit SYSTEM.INI and maximize the settings.

❶ Run SysEdit and select SYSTEM.INI to edit.

❷ Find the [386Enh] section, and make sure FileSysChange=false.

❸ Make sure ReservePageFrame=false.

Run a batch file, but stay in DOS

Normally, a batch file returns to Windows when it's finished, but this may not be what you want.

Run COMMAND.COM as the last command in the batch file.

Let's say you have a DOS 5.0 batch file that simply displays your memory allocation, and you want to stay in DOS when this batch file is finished.

❶ To create the batch file, open Notepad and type the following commands:

```
@echo off
mem/c | more
command
```

❷ Save this file with the name SHOWMEM.BAT.

Give each batch file an environment of its own

Some programs need a larger environment than the one they're normally allocated.

Start each program with COMMAND.COM specifying its own environment.

● Use the following command line to run a program and specify a larger environment.

COMMAND.COM /E:512 /C MYPROGRAM

In this example, the environment is 512 bytes, but you can substitute any number you'd like. MYPROGRAM can be any executable DOS file: EXE, COM, BAT, or PIF.

Run Windows in the right mode

If you're not running Windows in the right mode, you won't be getting the most from your system.

Use 386 enhanced mode unless you have a good reason not to.

- If you run lots of DOS applications, use 386 enhanced mode.

- If you need to multitask DOS applications, use 386 enhanced mode.

- If you need to use virtual memory, use 386 enhanced mode.

- If you don't need any of these features, use standard mode, and Windows will run about 20 percent faster.

Force Windows to run in any mode

When Windows runs, it selects the mode in which to run based on your equipment. This may not be the mode you want.

Force Windows to run in any mode by using command line switches.

- To start Windows in 386 enhanced mode, use WIN/3.

- To start Windows in standard mode, use WIN/S or WIN/2.

- To start Windows in real mode, use WIN/R. (This option is only available in Windows 3.0—not Windows 3.1.)

Your equipment must be able to support the mode you select.

Use SMARTDrive and configure it for top performance

Windows needs a disk cache, and SMARTDrive, which comes with Windows and DOS, is the most compatible choice. For top performance, it must be configured correctly, however.

Install SMARTDrive, and use the correct settings.

❶ If SMARTDrive isn't running on your system, put the line

DEVICE=C:\WINDOWS\SMARTDRV.SYS
in your CONFIG.SYS for Window 3.0, or put

C:\WINDOWS\SMARTDRV.EXE
in your AUTOEXEC.BAT for Windows 3.1.

❷ After the line that loads SMARTDrive, you need to specify two parameters. The first is the size of the cache outside Windows, and the second is the size of the cache when running Windows.

❸ If you have 2MB of RAM or less, set the first parameter to 1024 and the second to 512.

❹ If you have more than 2MB of RAM, set the first parameter to 1024 and the second to 1024. A larger cache probably won't improve your disk's performance.

❺ Set BUFFERS, in your CONFIG.SYS, to 10.

❻ Set FileSysChange=false and ReservePageFrame=false in SYSTEM.INI.

❼ Make sure your interleave is set correctly. Most modern hard disks can use 1:1 interleaves, which is the optimum.

❽ Defragment your hard drive using a commercial program.

❾ Use a permanent swap file.

Install a permanent swapfile

If you're using Windows' virtual memory and you're not using a permanent swapfile, you're not getting the fastest performance from your system.

Install a permanent swapfile.

For Windows 3.1

❶ Run Control Panel (on the Main group) and click on 386 Enhanced.

❷ Click on the Virtual Memory button.

❸ Under Type, select Permanent.

❹ Under Size, type in a value from 3072K to 8096K.

❺ Click on OK.

For Windows 3.0

❶ Run Windows in Real mode by typing WIN/R at the DOS prompt.

❷ Select File, Run, and type SWAPFILE in the text box.

❸ Select a size for your swapfile and reboot.

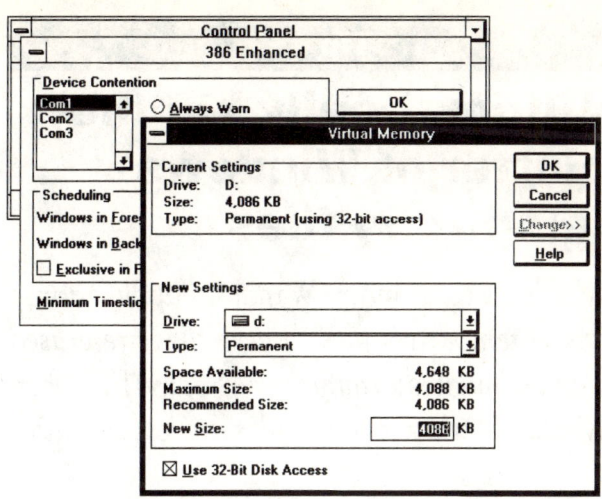

Use the 386 Enhanced section of Windows Control Panel to install a permanent swapfile.

Automatically kill the clutter of Windows' temporary files

Windows (and many Windows applications) create temporary files. These files are erased when Windows terminates normally. But when Windows crashes, these files are left to clutter up your disk.

Automatically erase any temporary files in your TEMP directory each time AUTOEXEC.BAT runs.

❶ Make sure you have the following two environment variables in your AUTOEXEC.BAT file:

SET TEMP=C:\WINDOWS\TEMP
SET TMP=C:\WINDOWS\TEMP

❷ Near the end of your AUTOEXEC.BAT file, add the line

ECHO Y | ERASE C:\WINDOWS\TEMP*.*
    >NUL

This will erase automatically any temp files remaining in your TEMP directory.

Double-time your mouse and keyboard

A sluggish keyboard or mouse can make com-puting a misery.

Adjust your Windows and DOS mouse and keyboard setting.

- To adjust your Windows mouse speed, run Control Panel, select Mouse, and move the speed bar three-fourths of the way to the right. Experiment from there.

- To adjust your Windows keyboard speed, run Control Panel, select Keyboard, and move the Delay and Repeat rate slider bars to the maximum—all the way to the right.

- To adjust your DOS mouse speed, add the switch /S55 to the line in your CONFIG.SYS or AUTOEXEC.BAT that installs your mouse driver and experiment from there.

- To adjust your DOS keyboard speed, add the line MODE CON DELAY=1 RATE=32 to your AUTOEXEC.BAT file.

To really enhance your mouse performance, upgrade to the Microsoft's Mouse 8.0 software.

Extend your path with SUBST

Almost every Windows (and DOS) application's installation program adds itself to your path. Before long your path will exceed the 127-character maximum.

Use DOS's SUBST command to create virtual drives, and add these to your path rather than long path names.

Let's say you have three directories that you want to add to your path, but your path is already 120 characters long. These directories are

    C:\UT\PCTOOLS
    C:\UT\WINFAX
    C:\WP\ALDUS

To add these three directories to your path normally would require 38 more characters.

❶ Run SysEdit and select your AUTOEXEC.BAT file to edit.

❷ Before your PATH statement, add the following commands:

    SUBST D: C:\UT\PCTOOLS
    SUBST E: C:\UT\WINFAX
    SUBST F: C:\WP\ALDUS

❸ Add the following drives to your path
D:,E:,F:

With SUBST, you can add the 38
characters needed for the three
directories to your path using just 8
characters.

❹ Reboot for your path changes to take
effect.

When you're installing new software, especially a new version of Windows, it's a good
idea to remove your SUBST mappings. To do
this, use the command SUBST *L: /D*, where L
is the drive letter to remove.

Save disk space by deleting unnecessary files

Windows requires a large investment in disk space, which you may not be able to afford.

Delete unnecessary files.

❶ Run File Manager and move to your Windows subdirectory.

❷ You can safely delete any of the following files, provided you don't need the applications.

*.BMP (These are bitmap files and are probably wallpaper).

*.SCR (These are Windows 3.1 screen saver files).

CALC.EXE, CALC.HLP (Calculator and its help file).

CALENDAR.EXE, CALENDAR.HLP (Calendar and its help file).

CARDFILE.EXE, CARDFILE.HLP (Cardfile and its help file).

CLOCK.EXE (Clock).

MSDOS.EXE (The MS-DOS Executive).

PBRUSH.EXE, PBRUSH.DLL, PBRUSH.HLP (Paintbrush, its DLL, and help file).

RECORDER.EXE, RECORDER.DLL, RECORDER.HLP (Recorder, its DLL, and help file).

REVERSI.EXE, REVERSI.HLP (Reversi and its help file that come with Windows 3.0).

WINMINE.EXE, WINMINE.HLP (Minesweeper and its help file that come with Windows 3.1)

SOL.EXE, SOL.HLP (Solitaire game with its help file).

TERMINAL.EXE, TERMINAL,HLP (Terminal and its help file).

WRITE.EXE, WRITE.HLP (Write and its help file).

Always use the latest version of the Microsoft drivers when you upgrade

Unless you're using the latest versions of the critical Microsoft drivers, Windows and most applications won't run at their best.

Always upgrade to the latest drivers when you install a new Microsoft product.

If you're offered new versions of the following drivers with a new version of Windows, DOS, or any Microsoft product, take them!

- MOUSE.SYS or MOUSE.COM. Even if you don't have a Microsoft mouse, if your mouse is Microsoft compatible, it will work with the Microsoft driver.

- SMARTDRV.EXE (formerly SMARTDRV.SYS). New versions of this disk cache come with Windows and DOS. Always use the latest version.

- HIMEM.SYS. This is the Microsoft high memory and extended memory manager. Always use the latest version.

- EMM386.EXE (formerly EMM386.SYS). This is Microsoft's expanded memory and upper memory manager. Use this to simulate expanded memory and to load TSRs and device drivers high on 386 machines. Always use the latest version.

Safeguard your program groups and initialization files

Application bugs or just plain rude installation programs can turn your groups and INI files into a scrambled mess.

Save your groups and INI files each time you boot your PC and before you install any new application.

❶ Run Notepad and enter the following lines

```
@echo off
echo Backing up INI files...
copy c:\windows\*.ini c:\windows\ini >nul
echo Backing up GRP files...
copy c:\windows\*.grp c:\windows\ini >nul
```

❷ Save this file with the name SAVEWIN.BAT.

❸ Create an INI subdirectory off your WINDOWS directory to store your saved INI and GRP files.

❹ Run this batch file before you install any new application.

❺ Also, run this batch file from your AUTOEXEC.BAT with the command CALL SAVEWIN.

Get the most from your load= and run= lines

The load= and run= lines have the same 127-character limit as your path statement.

Use Windows' Startup group to limit the entries on your load= and run= lines.

❶ Copy the icon for each application in your run= line to your Windows Startup group.

❷ Copy the icon for each application in your load= line to your Windows Startup group. Select the icon, choose File, Properties, and check Run Minimized.

❸ The Startup group is only available with Windows 3.1. If you're using an earlier version of Windows, you can save space on your load= and run= lines by specifying only the program name when the program is on your path. Specify full paths only when it's necessary.

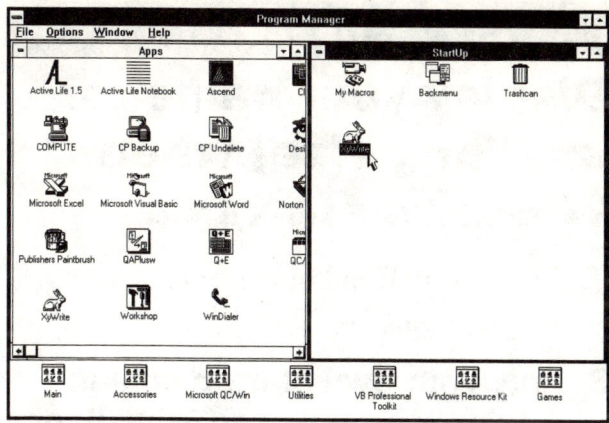

Copy the icon of each application you want to load or run at startup to your Startup group.

Display your name (or anything else) when Windows starts up

The Microsoft Windows startup screen gets boring pretty quickly.

Supply your own startup screen. (For this tip, you'll need WinGIF or some program that can save files in RLE format.)

❶ Rename you WIN.COM file WIN._OM.

❷ Open Paintbrush and select Option, Image Attributes.

❸ For Units, select Pels, and for Width and Height, choose 640 × 480.

❹ Create your startup screen, try to keep it simple, and save it.

❺ Run WinGIF, load your screen, and save it as an RLE image in your SYSTEM subdirectory.

❻ Run DOS Prompt and change to your SYSTEM subdirectory.

❼ Enter the following command:

COPY/B
    WIN.CNF+VGALOGO.LGO+*MYLOGO.RLE*
    WIN.COM

where *MYLOGO.RLE* is the name of RLE image you created.

❽ Copy your new WIN.COM file to your WINDOWS directory.

❾ Exit Windows and rerun it. You'll see your new startup screen.

Display any screen when Windows starts up.

Skip the Microsoft brag screen at startup

Microsoft's startup screen can become boring (as can one you've created yourself).

Skip the startup screen.

● Instead of typing WIN or WIN/s, where s is a switch, type WIN : or WIN/s : to bypass the startup screen.

This works with the original WIN.COM or a new WIN.COM you create yourself (see Tip #66).

Reinstall any Windows program without running Setup

Often you need to reinstall just one program, file, or group of files from the Windows distribution disk. Usually you can't do this without reinstalling all of Windows again.

Learn to decompress the files on the Windows distribution disks.

❶ Find the EXPAND.EXE program on the Windows distribution disks. (It will probably be on disk 1 or 2.)

❷ Copy this file to your WINDOWS subdirectory.

❸ You'll notice that most of the other files on the disk have extensions that end with an underscore (_), for example WINHELP.EX_, MOUSE.DR_, and so on. These are compressed files. (Note that in early versions of Windows, the compressed files end in EXE, but they are not executable.)

❹ To uncompress one of these files, for example WINHELP.EX_, type

**EXPAND A:WINHELP.EX_
    C:\WINDOWS\WINHELP.EXE**

C:\WINDOWS\WINHELP.EXE is the executable file you're creating.

(Your source and destination drives may be different from A and C used above.)

Change the default icon title font

Windows default font for icon titles can be hard to read.

If you have Windows 3.1, you can substitute a different font for the default.

❶ Run SysEdit, select WIN.INI.

❷ Find the [desktop] section, and insert the lines

    IconTitleFaceName=*Fontname*
    IconTitleSize=*Fontsize*

where *Fontname* is the name of a font on your system and *Fontsize* is the size, in points, you want to use.

A good choice for an alternative to the default 8-point MS Sans Serif is the System font (which is only available in 10-point). To make System the title font, your lines would look like this:

    IconTitleFaceName=System
    IconTitleSize=10

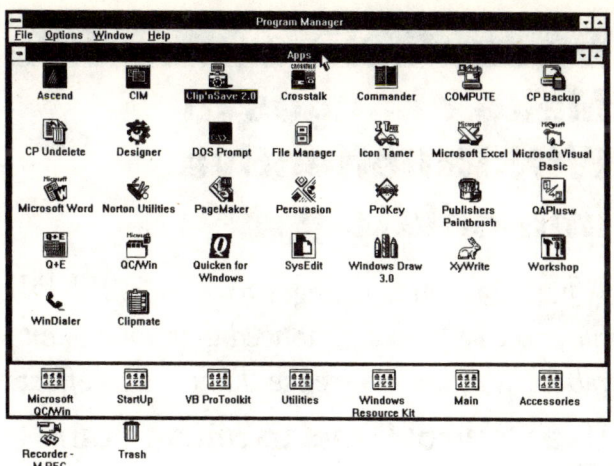

If the default icon title font is too small, replace it with the System font.

Make changes in WIN.INI effective immediately

When you make changes to your WIN.INI file, you've probably noticed that you have to reboot Windows to see the changes take effect.

Use Control Panel to reload your WIN.INI without rebooting.

❶ Make some changes to your WIN.INI file. For example, you might want to add an extension to the [Extensions] section.

❷ To make the change current without rerunning Windows, run Control Panel, double-click on Desktop, and click on OK. This will reread your WIN.INI file and make most of your changes current.

You can use almost any Control Panel icon to update your changes. This technique doesn't work with all WIN.INI parameters, however. Color is the most important exception.

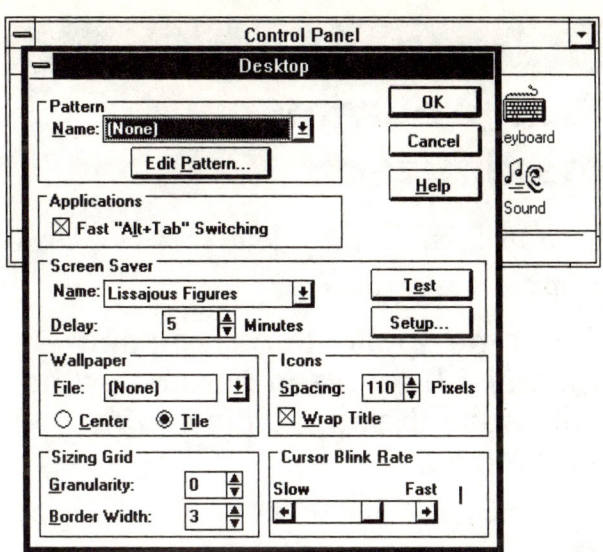

Click on OK in Control Panel's Desktop to make changes to your WIN.INI effective immediately.

Run programs maximized

Each application in Windows seems to choose its initial size at random.

For some applications, you can specify a Maximized parameter that will cause the application to run maximized.

❶ Run SysEdit and select WIN.INI.

❷ Go to the [Terminal] section.

❸ Put the line Maximized=1 in the [Terminal] section.

❹ Use Control Panel to make your change effective (see Tip #70).

Not all applications support this parameter. Some apps that do are Terminal (undocumented), Excel, Q+E, and Crosstalk. This technique does not work with PageMaker or WinWord.

Run a program and maximize it with Recorder

Often times you'll want to run a program maximized, but the program doesn't support the WIN.INI Maximized parameter described in Tip #71.

Use Recorder to run the program.

❶ Run Recorder and make sure Ignore Mouse is selected under Options, Preferences.

❷ Let's say the application you want to run maximized is Paintbrush. Start recording and in Program Manager, select File, Run, and type PBRUSH in the text box.

❸ When Paintbrush appears, press Alt-Space to call the Control menu.

❹ Press x to maximize Paintbrush.

❺ Stop recording, choose a hotkey (Ctrl-Alt-P is a good choice), and save your macro.

● To have Recorder kill itself, use the technique found in Tip #37.

● To run a specific macro with Recorder, see Tip #91.

Don't use Windows wallpaper

Wallpaper is neat, and although it can be fun, it slows your system down and uses memory.

Don't use wallpaper.

❶ Run Control Panel (on the Main group).

❷ Double-click on Desktop.

❸ Under Wallpaper, select None.

❹ Click on Color.

❺ Select a pleasing color for your background.

Determine Windows' mode when you use an alternate shell

If you're using an alternate shell, you may not be able to tell which mode Windows is running in.

Use WINVER.EXE.

❶ Select File, Run (or select any other means your shell offers to run a program).

❷ Type WINVER.EXE in the text box, and press Enter.

With Windows 3.1, you're never far from mode, memory, and resource information. The About dialog box in every 3.1 accessory (including Program Manager and File Manager) displays this information.

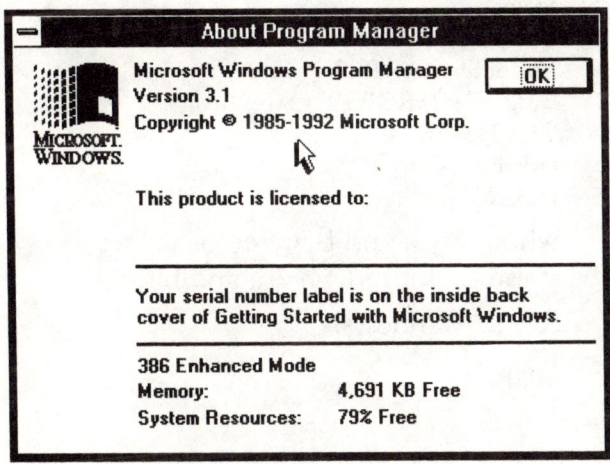

The About dialog box in every Windows 3.1 accessory displays system information.

Change the colors of buttons, highlight, and Help

The default colors for buttons, highlights, and Help may not be the best choices for you.

Change these colors with Control Panel and WIN.INI.

For Windows 3.1

❶ Run Control Panel (on the Main group), and double-click on Color.

❷ Select Color Palette.

❸ Click on highlight or button to change those colors.

For Windows 3.0

❶ Add the following lines to your WIN.INI file:

[colors]
ButtonFace=RGB
ButtonShadow=RGB
ButtonText=RGB
GrayText=RGB
Hilight=RGB
HilightText=RGB

where R, G, and B are color values standing for red, green, and blue.

❷ Rerun Windows.

For Windows 3.0 and 3.1

❶ Add the following lines to the [Windows Help] your WIN.INI file:

Jumpcolor=RGB
Popupcolor=RGB

❷ Rerun Windows.

Here are some useful values for R, G, and B.

Color	R	G	B
Black	0	0	0
Red	255	0	0
Green	0	255	0
Yellow	255	255	0
Blue	0	0	255
Magenta	255	0	255
Cyan	0	255	255
White	255	255	255

Print a Windows screen

There's no print-screen key in Windows.

Use Paintbrush and a Recorder macro to simulate this key.

❶ Grab your screen with Print Screen or Alt-Print Screen.

❷ Run Recorder and begin recording your macro.

❸ Run Paintbrush, and make the work area the correct size for your image.

❹ Paste the image into Paintbrush.

❺ Choose File, Print.

❻ Close Paintbrush.

❼ Save your Recorder macro.

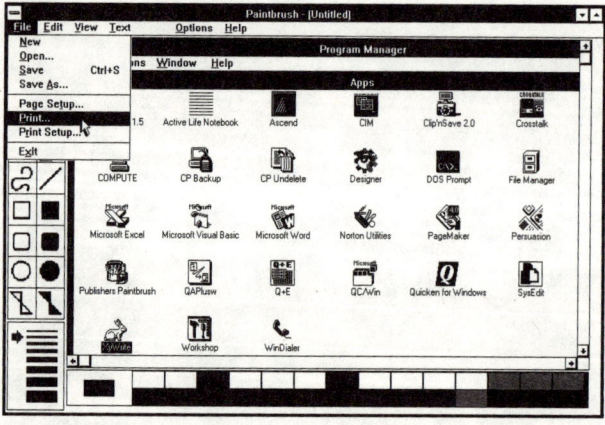

To print a Windows screen, paste it into Paintbrush, and print it.

Make your Windows and DOS apps run more smoothly

The default Timeslice setting for Windows is fine for a 16-MHz 386SX, but if you have a faster machine, you'll get better performance by changing it.

Change your Timeslice from the default of 20 to a lower number.

This will make applications run more smoothly in the foreground while you're doing something intensive in the background.

❶ Run Control Panel (on the Main group).

❷ Double-click on 386 Enhanced.

❸ As a starting point, change Timeslice from 20 to 5, 10, or 15, and experiment.

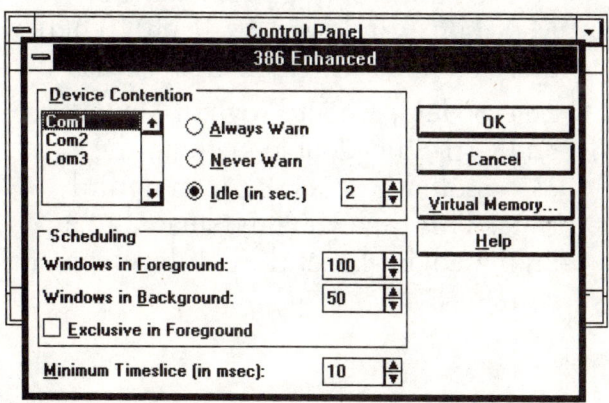

A Timeslice of 20 may not be the best value for your system.

See Windows' designers' names

You'll never be regarded as a Windows wizard until you know how to call up the Windows designer screen.

Learn the secret mouse clicks and keystrokes.

Windows 3.1

❶ Select Help, About Program Manager, and Ctrl-Shift-double-click on the Microsoft Windows flag icon. Nothing will happen this time. Click on OK.

❷ Select Help, About Program Manager, and Ctrl-Shift-double-click on the Microsoft Windows flag icon a second time. This time you'll see an animated, waving flag and the text "Dedicated to all the hard-working people of the Microsoft Windows 3.10 Team!" There's more to come. Click on OK.

❸ Select Help, About Program Manager, and Ctrl-Shift-double-click on the Microsoft Windows flag icon a third time. This time you'll be treated to an animated display of the 3.1 development team.

Windows 3.0

❶ Minimize all the apps on your desktop, and press and hold down F3.

❷ While holding F3, type win3.

❸ Release F3.

❹ Press Backspace.

❺ Click a mouse button to remove the screen.

The Windows 3.1 gang screen is an animated display in the About Program Manager dialog box.

Make sense of Windows' file extensions

Windows uses a large number of file types. You need to know the basic ones.

Learn the most important file extensions.

Here's a list of the most important file extensions used or created by Windows and Windows applications.

BMP	Bitmapped image for Paintbrush.
CRD	Cardfile data.
DLL	Dynamic Linked Library. Shared executable code.
DRV	Device driver.
EXE	Executable file.
FON	Font.
GRP	Program Manager group.
HLP	Help data file.
INI	Initialization file.
PIF	Program Information File. Configurations for DOS programs.
REC	Recorder macro file.
SCR	Screen saver file.
SYD	Backup file created by SysEdit.
SYS	Device driver.
TRM	Terminal telecommunications file.
TXT	Text file.
WRI	Write document.

Create your own double-click popup

With Windows, you don't need TSRs, but occasionally it's nice to have an application pop up with a keypress or mouse click.

Replace Task Manager with a different Windows application.

Let's say you want Calculator to be a mouse click (or keypress) away.

❶ Rename TASKMAN.EXE to TASKMAN._XE.

❷ Copy CALC.EXE TO TASKMAN.EXE.

❸ Each time you double-click on the desktop or press Ctrl-Esc (actions that usually call Task Manager), you'll run Calculator.

❹ To undo this change, rename TASKMAN._XE to TASKMAN.EXE.

You can also replace Task Manager by altering the taskman.exe= line in SYSTEM.INI. To substitute Calculator for Task Manager using this method, you'd replace

taskman.exe=taskman.exe

with

taskman.exe=calc.exe

Close any program window, and most document windows, with a double-click

Using menus to exit an application or close a document window is slow.

Double-click on the control-menu box, or press Alt-F4.

- To close any window, double-click on the Control-menu box in the upper-left corner of the window.

- To close an application window with the keyboard, press Alt-F4.

- To close a document window with the keyboard, press Ctrl-F4.

You can double-click on a restored document window to close it, but sometimes, depending on the application, you can't double-click on a maximized document window to close. Ctrl-F4 works, however.

Double-click here to
close an application
window.

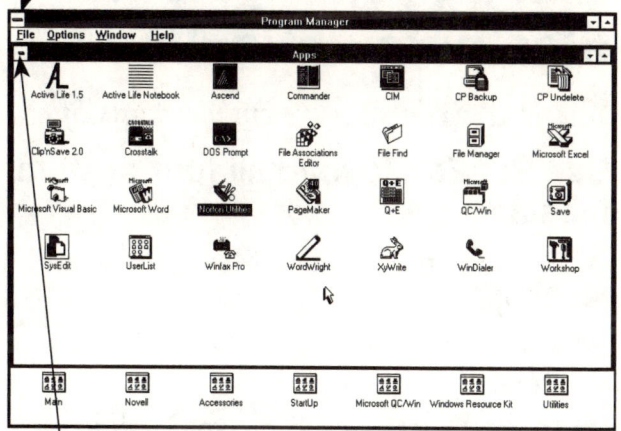

Double-click here to
close a document
window.

Call all your system files automatically

You need to edit your system files fairly often.

Use SysEdit to load all four system files at once.

❶ Activate the Program Manager's Main group.

❷ Choose File, New, and select Program Item.

❸ In the Description box, type SysEdit.

❹ In the Command Line box, type SYSEDIT.EXE.

❺ Click on OK and SysEdit's icon will appear on the group.

❻ Double-click on the icon to run the program, which loads your SYSTEM.INI, WIN.INI, CONFIG.SYS, and AUTOEXEC.BAT files.

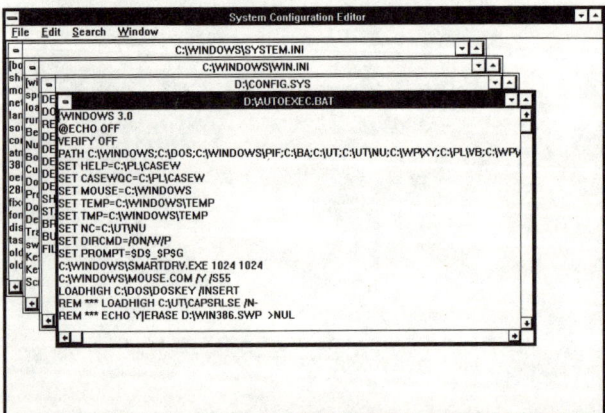

Use SysEdit to edit all four system files.

Install Windows' Help application

Help is available from most Windows applications, but it's often more convenient to access help from Program Manager.

Install Help on Program Manager.

❶ In Program Manager, select Files, New, and Program Item.

❷ In the Description box, type Windows Help.

❸ In the Command Line box, type WINHELP.EXE.

❹ Double-click on the Help icon anytime to run help. Then choose File, Open to open any application's help file.

All Windows help files end with an HLP extension.

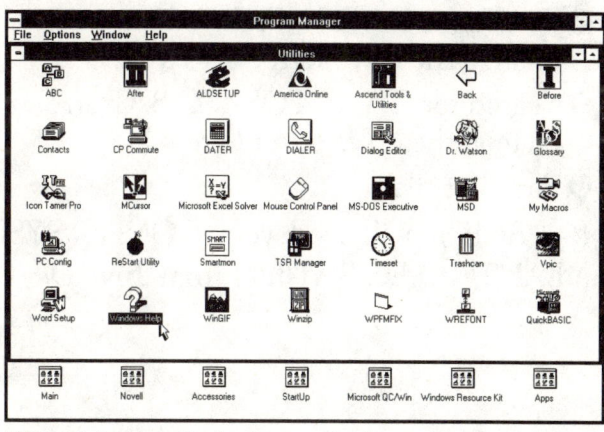

With Help installed on your desktop, it's easy to call any app's help file.

Change SysEdit's default files

SysEdit always looks for the same four system files, and it always looks on drive C. There's no option to change that.

Edit the SYSEDIT.EXE file with Write.

Let's say your system files reside on drive D (if you're using Stacker, for example), and you want SysEdit to load your CONFIG.SYS and AUTOEXEC.BAT files from the D drive.

❶ Copy SYSEDIT.EXE (found in your SYSTEM subdirectory) to SYSEDIT._XE, so you'll have a backup.

❷ Run Write, choose File, Open, and type in \SYSTEM\SYSEDIT.EXE.

❸ When prompted, select No Conversion.

❹ Search for C:\CONFIG.SYS and change the drive letter C to a D.

❺ Search for C:\AUTOEXEC.BAT and change the drive letter C to a D.

❻ Save the file.

Now SysEdit will load your CONFIG.SYS and AUTOEXEC.BAT files from drive D.

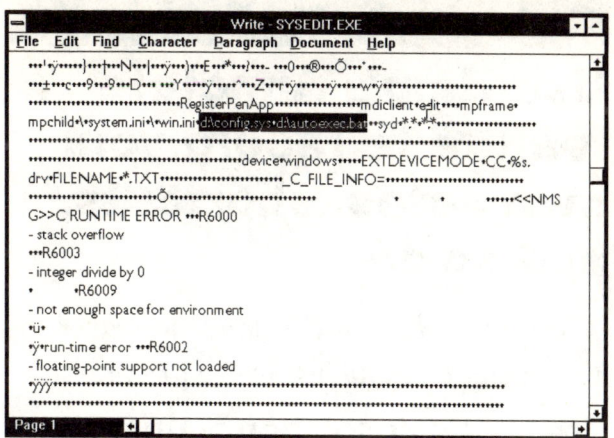

To change SysEdit's default drives for AUTOEXEC.BAT and CONFIG.SYS, load SYSEDIT.EXE directly into Write and edit it.

Use Help's Annotate feature to record your own notes, shortcuts, and so on

When you find a neat Windows shortcut or tip, it's difficult to know just where to store it.

Use Help's annotation feature to record your notes.

❶ Open the help file for any application.

❷ Select Edit, Annotate.

❸ In the text window, type in your annotation and click on Save.

A paperclip will appear on the page to remind you that you have an annotation.

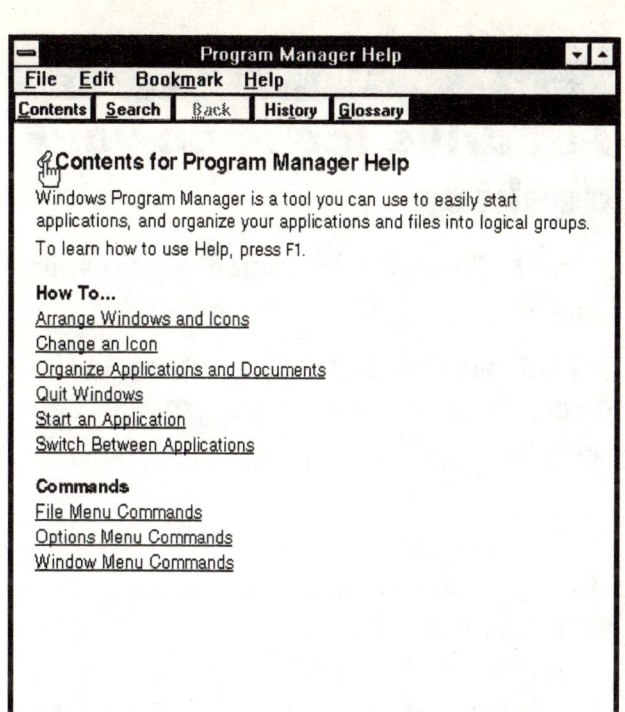

Contents for Program Manager Help

Windows Program Manager is a tool you can use to easily start applications, and organize your applications and files into logical groups.

To learn how to use Help, press F1.

How To...

Arrange Windows and Icons

Change an Icon

Organize Applications and Documents

Quit Windows

Start an Application

Switch Between Applications

Commands

File Menu Commands

Options Menu Commands

Window Menu Commands

The paperclip indicates that this page of help contains an annotation.

Put drive icons on your desktop

Almost all systems have multiple drives, and switching among these takes time.

Install an MS-DOS Executive for each drive on your system.

❶ In Program Manger, select File, New, Program item.

❷ In Description, type Drive C.

❸ In Command Line, type

C:\MSDOS.EXE

❹ For drives A, B, and any others, substitute A, B, or any other letter for C in number 3.

MS-DOS Executive can be used to place disk drive icons on the desktop.

Undo your last selection

No one's perfect.

Most Windows applications let you undo your last deletion with Alt-Backspace.

❶ In Notepad (which supports undo), type in some text for a test.

❷ Delete a portion of the text.

❸ Press Alt-Backspace, and your text will reappear.

Find the best Windows online resources

There is a wealth of excellent shareware and freeware Windows programs, but you have to know where to look.

Learn the best places to find Windows stuff.

● On CompuServe, there are several forums:

Windows New
Windows Advanced
Windows Applications A
Windows Applications B
Windows Applications C
Microsoft Basic (for Visual Basic)
Microsoft Operating Systems
Microsoft Languages (for Quick C for Windows)
Microsoft SDK (for the Software Development Kit)

● On GEnie, two round tables house the majority of the Windows files:

IBM PC Round Table
Microsoft Round Table

Learn the five ways to close an application

Most people know one or two ways to close Windows applications, but there are many, and knowing all of them means you'll always be able to use the quickest.

Learn the five magic ways to end a Windows app.

- Choose File, Exit from the menu bar.
- Choose the Control menu and select Close.
- Double-click on Control box.
- Call Task Manager, select the program, and choose End task.
- Press Alt-F4.

Learn the six ways to run a program

Most people know one or two ways to run an application, but there are many, and knowing all of them means you'll always be able to use the quickest.

Learn the six magic ways to run a Windows app.

- Double-click on the program's icon in Program Manager.
- Double-click on an associated document's icon in Program Manager.
- Double-click on the program's filename in File Manager or MS-DOS Executive.
- Double-click on an associated document's filename in File Manager or MS-DOS Executive.
- Select File, Run from Program Manager, File Manager, or MS-DOS Executive, and type the program's name.
- Select File, Run from Program Manager, File Manager, or MS-DOS Executive, and type an associated document's name.

Run a specific Recorder macro

Many times, you want to run one single macro in a Recorder file.

Use Recorder's hotkey switch.

❶ Make sure your macro specifies a hotkey.

❷ On the command line, put RECORDER -h *hotkey filename.ext*, where *filename.ext* is name of the Recorder macro and *hotkey* is the key combination that normally runs the macro.

For the hotkey, use the following symbols, plus the key name.

Key	Symbol
Alt	%
Ctrl	^
Shift	+

As an example, if your hotkey is Shift-F10 and your macro file is named MYMACROS.REC, the command would be

RECORDER -h +F10 MYMACROS.REC

Run a Recorder macro at Windows startup

To run a single Recorder macro, you need to specify parameters. This is impossible with load= and run= in WIN.INI—you can only type a single filename.

Use the Association command and Recorder's hotkey switch for Windows 3.0 or use the Startup group for Windows 3.1.

Windows 3.0

❶ Name the Recorder file that contains the macro with a unique extension, such as your initials.

❷ Associate the file with your initials as its extension and the Recorder command with the -h switch. For example, if Ctrl-A is your hotkey, and the file is MYMACROS.CK, the association would be RECORDER -h ^A for the extension CK.

❸ Place the associated MYMACROS.CK file in your WIN.INI. When Windows boots, your macro will run.

Windows 3.1

❶ Select the Startup group and select File, New, Program Item.

❷ In the Description text box, type in Startup Macros, or something similar.

❸ In the Command Line text box, type RECORDER -h *hotkey* MACROS.REC, where *hotkey* is your hotkey combination and MACROS.REC is the name of your macro file.

❹ If, for example, your hotkey is Ctrl-Alt-Shift-x and your macro file is MYMACROS.REC, you'd put RECORDER -h %^+x M.REC in the text box.

❺ Check Run Minimized, and click on OK to save your macro.

See parent directories on a Novell network

When you run Windows on a Novell network, you don't see the double dots (..) in directory listings that allow you to move to the parent directory.

Place SHOW DOTS = ON in SHELL.CFG.

❶ Using Notepad, or another text editor, load SHELL.CFG (or NET.CFG).

❷ Add the line SHOW DOTS = ON.

❸ Logoff the network and reboot.

Stop receiving those annoying broadcast messages on a Novell network

When you're running Windows on a network and you receive a broadcast message, you have to stop what you're working on, read the message, and click on OK.

Disable broadcast messages.

❶ Run Control Panel and double-click on Network.

❷ Click on Messages disabled.

❸ Click on OK.

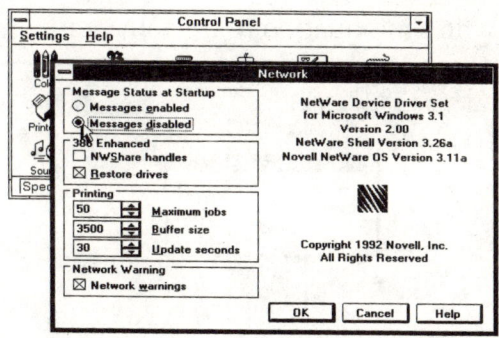

Use Control Panel's Network option to disable broadcast messages.

Copy disks with File Manager

Making a copy of a disk with the same drive using DOS's DISKCOPY command is a long process that usually involves swapping disks several times.

Use the 3.1 File Manager's Copy Disk command.

● Run File Manager, select Disk, Copy Disk, and follow directions.

The File Manager's copy option almost always copies a disk in a single pass, even when copying 1.44MB floppies. The progress dialog moves from 1 to 49 percent while the program copies the source disk and from 50 to 100 percent while it writes information to the target disk.

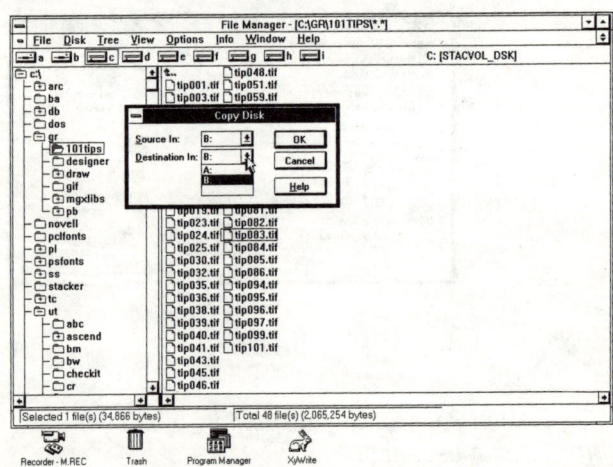

You can use File Manager's Copy Disk command to copy floppies in one pass.

Edit PROGMAN.INI

One morning you boot Windows and one or all of your groups are lost.

Learn to edit PROGMAN.INI.

❶ Run Notepad and load PROGMAN.INI (in your WINDOWS subdirectory).

❷ The file has two sections, [Settings] and [Groups], with the following form:

```
[Settings]
Window=-4 0 801 528 1
SaveSettings=1
[Groups]
Order= 7 1 5 4 3 2 8
Group1=C:\WINDOWS\MAIN.GRP
Group2=C:\WINDOWS\ACCESSOR.GRP
Group3=C:\WINDOWS\GAMES.GRP
Group4=C:\WINDOWS\STARTUP.GRP
Group7=C:\WINDOWS\UTILITIE.GRP
Group5=C:\WINDOWS\QCWIN.GRP
Group8=C:\WINDOWS\APPS.GRP
```

❸ If your groups are still in your Windows subdirectory, but they don't appear in PROGMAN.INI, simply add them, following the form where n is the number of the group.

```
Groupn=C:\WINDOWS\GROUPNAME.GRP
```

Master Windows lingo

Unless you know the basic Windows jargon, you'll be lost reading the documentation, references like this book, or online help.

Learn the key words and their meanings.

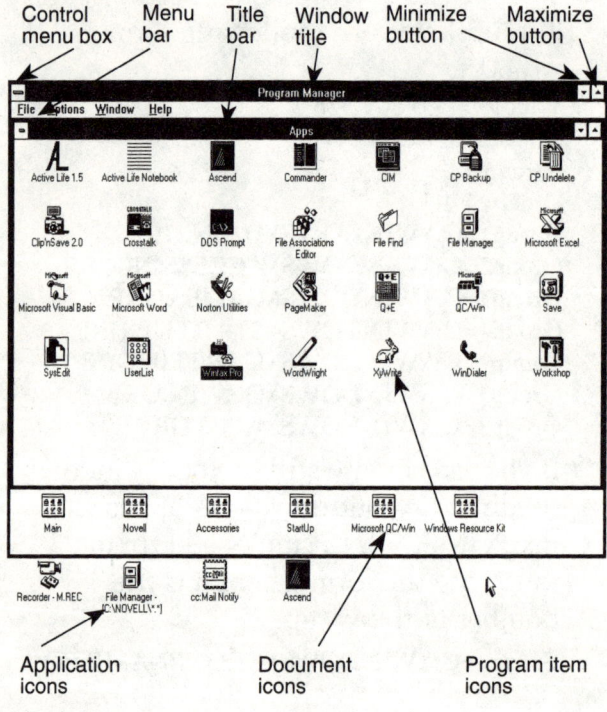

Control menu box · Menu bar · Title bar · Window title · Minimize button · Maximize button

Application icons · Document icons · Program item icons

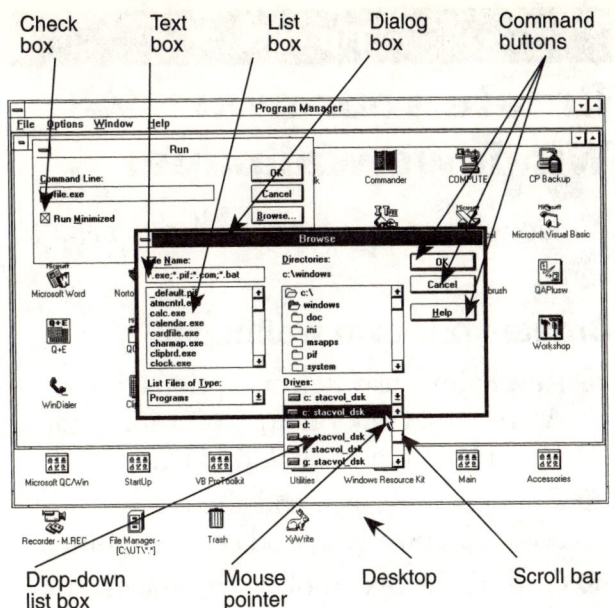

Check box   Text box   List box   Dialog box   Command buttons

Drop-down list box   Mouse pointer   Desktop   Scroll bar

Create your own Windows wallpaper

Windows' default solid-color desktop can be boring.

Create your own wallpaper.

❶ Run Paintbrush, select Options, Image Attributes, click on *in*, type 1 for Width, 1 for Height, and click on OK.

❷ Choose a font face and size (Helvetica bold, 12 point is a good starting point).

❸ Choose the text tool (the one with the abc in the box), and type your name, your company's name, or anything else you'd like in the box.

❹ Save the file.

❺ Run Control Panel (on the Main group) and select Desktop.

❻ Under Wallpaper, choose your creation.

❼ Select Tile, and click on OK.

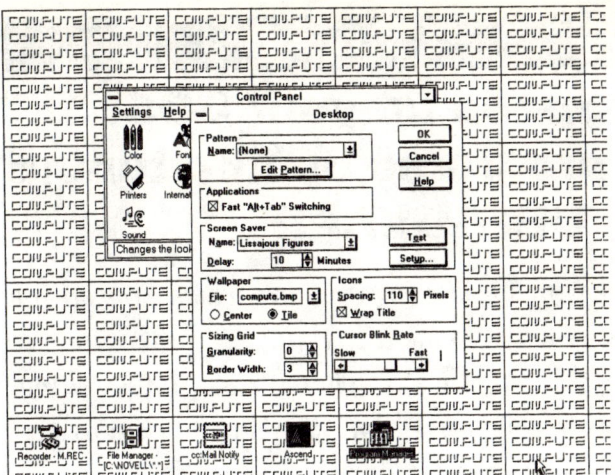

Create your own personalized Windows wallpaper with Paintbrush and install it with Control Panel, Desktop.

Speed up your DOS programs by fine tuning _DEFAULT.PIF

Every DOS program, for which you do not explicitly create a PIF file, uses the setting in _DEFAULT.PIF when it runs. If the settings aren't optimized for your machine, your performance will suffer.

Edit _DEFAULT.PIF.

❶ Run PIF Editor (on the Accessories group), and load _DEFAULT.PIF. This file will be in either the WINDOWS or SYSTEM subdirectory.

❷ For EMS Memory and XMS Memory, make sure all values are 0.

❸ Full Screen should be checked.

❹ Neither Background nor Exclusive should be checked.

❺ Close Window on Exit should be checked.

❻ Click on the Advanced button.

❼ Change Foreground Priority to 1000. Values up to 10,000 are allowed. You may want to experiment with higher values.

❽ Detect Idle Time, All Memory Options, and All Monitor Ports should be unchecked.

❾ Emulate Text Mode should be checked.

❿ All Other Options should be unchecked.

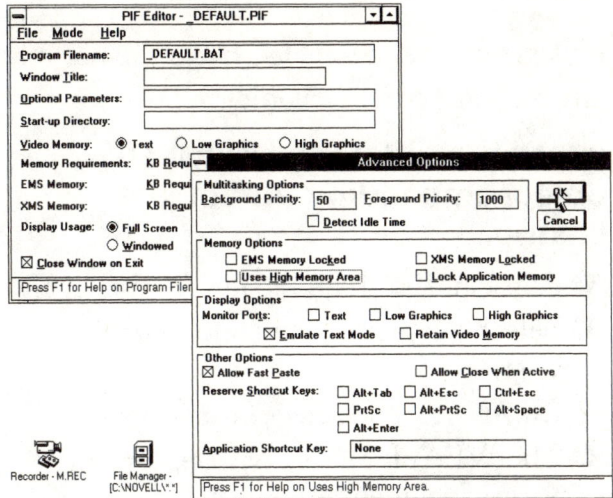

By fine tuning your _DEFAULT.PIF, you'll improve the performance of all your DOS programs that don't have their own PIF.

Learn to use OLE

Unless you understand OLE, you're not getting the most from Windows 3.1.

Learn the difference between object embedding and object linking.

❶ Run Paintbrush and load WEAVE.BMP.

❷ Select the picture, and choose Edit, Copy.

❸ Run Write, and select Edit, Paste.

❹ The WEAVE picture will appear in your Write document. You've created an embedded object.

❺ Close Paintbrush.

❻ Double-click on the WEAVE object. Paintbrush will run with WEAVE.BMP loaded.

❼ To link an object, follow all the steps above, except for step 3, choose Edit, Paste Link.

Notes:

● When you embed an object, you create a static copy of the object. If the original changes, your copy won't change. When you link an object, you create a dynamic copy of the object. When the original changes, so does the copy.

● The Packager application that comes with Windows 3.1 lets your embed objects, but allows you to display them as icons.

Create a macro to display a long file listing in File Manager

File Manager's default window displays lots of files, but no file details. Often this is fine, but many times it's essential to know a file's creation date, its attributes, or both.

Create macros to toggle File Manager's file listing between a window that shows all file details and one that displays a short listing.

❶ With File Manager on your desktop, start recording.

❷ Press Alt-V, A (Press Alt-V, F for Windows 3.0).

❸ Stop recording.

A good key combination for this macro is Ctrl-Alt-L (for long).

A macro to return to the short listing is just as easy to create.

❶ Again, with File Manager on your desktop, start recording.

❷ Press Alt-V, N.

❸ Stop recording.

A good key combination for this macro is Ctrl-Alt-S (for short).

Where to find more Windows information

After you master the basics, it's not what you know that's important, it's knowing where to find what you need.

Learn the top Windows references.

● *Running Windows*, Stinson and Andrews (Microsoft Press; $24.95).

An excellent book for intermediate users, this volume begins where *Windows 3.1 Companion* leaves off.

● *Windows Resource Kit* (Microsoft, $19.95).

This one's essential. It offers in-depth technical information you won't find anywhere else. The accompanying disk has several useful utilities including monitors for SMARTDrive and system resources.

● *Windows 3.1 Companion*, Lorenz and O'Mara (Microsoft Press; $27.95).

A good place to start, this is perhaps the best Windows book for beginners.

● *Windows 3.1 Power Tools*, The LeBlond Group (Bantam; $49.95).

This huge book contains an amazing amount of information on Windows, especially on how to configure Windows.

- *Windows 3.1 Secrets*, Brian Livingston (IDG Books; $39.95).

  From one of the top Windows gurus, there's something interesting or useful on almost every page.

Index

About the Author

CLIFTON KARNES has been programming and writing about computers since 1982. After completing a Masters Degree in Music Theory, he studied programming at the undergraduate and graduate levels and has programmed mainframes, minicomputers, and micros in C, Pascal, Assembly Language, BASIC, COBOL, and Forth.

Clifton joined COMPUTE Publications in 1987 and is currently Editor of *COMPUTE Magazine*. He writes "Point & Click," the magazine's Windows column, and has published more than 100 articles on Windows, DOS utilities, productivity software, and programming—his four main interests.

He lives in Greensboro, North Carolina with his wife Sharon and son Jeffrey.

Technical Note

The primary research for this book was done on two Gateway 2000 25-MHz 386 computers. One of the machines was equipped with 8MB or RAM, a 60MB ESDI hard disk (transformed into a 120MB drive with Stacker AT/16), and was connected to a Novell network running Netware 3.11. The other machine had 4MB of RAM and a 120MB ESDI hard disk (transformed into a 220MB drive with Stacker AT/16). Both machines ran Windows 3.1, Windows 3.0, DOS 5.0, and both had Super VGA graphics systems.

The manuscript was prepared using XyWrite, screen shots were captured using Clip'nSave, and both were submitted to COMPUTE Books in electronic form.

101 Essential Tips Series

101 Essential Windows Tips
Clifton Karnes

101 Essential Word for Windows Tips
Herbert Tyson

101 Essential Excel for Windows Tips
Jan Altman (Available July 1992)